HUMAN RIGHTS

GLOBAL C⊕NNECTIⰙNS

America's Role in a Changing World
Changing Climates
The Changing Global Economy
Environment and Natural Resources
Feeding a Hungry World
The Human Population
Human Rights
One World or Many?
Pandemics and Global Health
Terrorism and Security

GLOBAL

CONNECTIONS

HUMAN RIGHTS

DOUGLAS A. PHILLIPS
SERIES EDITOR: CHARLES F. GRITZNER

CHELSEA HOUSE
PUBLISHERS
An imprint of Infobase Publishing

This book is dedicated to my friends, colleagues, and others on six continents who have had their human rights stolen or denied. I honor your courage, compassion, and conviction and your continuing efforts to protect the rights of others—even those who perpetrated the violation of your rights. May these transgressors be brought to the justice that you were denied.

Human Rights

Copyright © 2009 by Infobase Publishing

Chelsea House
An imprint of Infobase Publishing
132 West 31st Street
New York, NY 10001

Library of Congress Cataloging-in-Publication Data
Phillips, Douglas A.
  Human rights / by Douglas A. Phillips ; consulting editor Charles F. Gritzner.
     p. cm. — (Global connections)
  Includes bibliographical references and index.
  ISBN 978-1-60413-286-1 (hardcover)
  1. Human rights--Juvenile literature. I. Gritzner, Charles F. II. Title. III. Series.
  JC571.P455 2009
  323—dc22   2008054882

Chelsea House books are available at special discounts when purchased in bulk quantities for businesses, associations, institutions, or sales promotions. Please call our Special Sales Department in New York at (212) 967-8800 or (800) 322-8755.

You can find Chelsea House on the World Wide Web
at http://www.chelseahouse.com

Text design by Annie O'Donnell
Cover design by Takeshi Takahashi

Printed in the United States of America

Bang EJB 10 9 8 7 6 5 4 3 2 1

This book is printed on acid-free paper.

All links and Web addresses were checked and verified to be correct at the time of publication. Because of the dynamic nature of the Web, some addresses and links may have changed since publication and may no longer be valid.

CONTENTS

INTRODUCTION

A GLOBAL COMMUNITY

Globalization is the process of coming together as a closely connected global community. It began thousands of years ago, when tribal groups and small hunting parties wandered from place to place. The process accelerated following Columbus's epic voyage more than five centuries ago. Europeans—an estimated 50 million of them—spread out to occupy lands throughout the world. This migration transformed the distribution of the world's peoples and their cultures forever. In the United States and Canada, for example, most people speak a West European language. Most practice a religious faith with roots in the ancient Middle East and eat foods originating in Asia.

Today, we are citizens of a closely interwoven global community. Events occurring half a world away can be watched and experienced, often as they happen, in our own homes. People, materials, and even diseases can be transported from continent to continent in a single day, thanks to jet planes. Electronic communications make possible the instantaneous exchange of information by phone, e-mail, or other means with friends or business associates almost anywhere in the world. Trade and commerce, perhaps more so than any other aspect of our daily lives, amply illustrate the importance of global linkages. How many things in your home (including your clothing) are of international origin? What foods and beverages have you consumed today that came from other lands? Could Northern America's economy survive without foreign oil, iron ore, copper, or other vital resources?

The GLOBAL CONNECTIONS series is designed to help you realize how closely people and places are tied to one another within the expanding global community. Each book introduces you to political, economic, environmental, social, medical, and other timely issues, problems, and prospects. The authors and editors hope you enjoy and learn from these books. May they hand you a passport to intellectual travels throughout our fascinating, complex, and increasingly "intradependent" world!

—*Charles F. Gritzner*
Series Editor

WHY SHOULD WE INVESTIGATE HUMAN RIGHTS?

Our journey into understanding human rights begins with a simple definition. Human rights are the rights and freedoms that all people are entitled to simply because they are human. Human rights affect you, your friends, your family, and distant people around the world every day. Although this definition seems simple, it represents very complex ideas. It is these ideas that this book will carefully explain in the following pages.

The application of human rights to societies has often been horrid. One hundred and fifty million is a number that you may want to remember. It is a number that will burn itself upon your soul when you know what it represents. What this number represents will be explained later in this chapter.

"HUMAN WRONGS"

Human rights are necessary because of the many human "wrongs" that have been committed throughout history. These human wrongs are many and always tragic. They include such things as children forced into labor, slavery, and unequal pay and access to jobs. Political persecution, discrimination, torture, and death also are included. History is littered with tales of human wrongs committed by despots, dictators, and even demo-cratically elected leaders. Adolf Hitler, Joseph Stalin, Osama bin Laden, and others have scarred the pages of history with their crimes against humanity. But not only political leaders are involved. Religion has been used as a justification for committing human wrongs against women, aboriginal peoples, and others. There are far too many examples of these wrongdoings to be listed on these pages.

Human wrongs are not just memories of the distant past. Many wrongs against people are still being committed today around the world. Political prisoners suffer when jailed and are often tortured for their political beliefs. Journalists are per-secuted for exposing the truth. Many women suffer because of religion and other aspects of their culture. Many aboriginal (native) peoples have lost their lands and cultural dignity. Some people cannot move freely. Others are forced to move against their wishes. Opponents of ruling political parties are often jailed without charges or trials. An estimated 800 million people are suffering from hunger. Human wrongs are still very widespread today—surprisingly even in the United States, Canada, Australia, New Zealand, and Western Europe.

HUMAN RIGHTS FOR ALL

Who has human rights? The answer is very simple according to the United Nations and most national constitutions. It is all peo-ple. If *anyone* fails to have the rights guaranteed by a society, then *no one* really possesses them. If, for example, a leader operates above the law, the citizens of that place are not guaranteed legal protection under the law. The rule of law exists when no person in a society is above the law. Everyone is subject to following the rules of a society, even presidents. Such conditions exist in the United States, Canada, Australia, and other democracies.

A system called the rule of man exists in places where political parties or leaders rule without following their country's laws. In other words, some people consider themselves to be above the laws of the society. This is certainly unfair and presents a system where human rights are violated in major ways. Countries like Myanmar

THE HUMAN TRAGEDY CALLED ETHNIC CLEANSING

The phrase *ethnic cleansing* sounds so, well, clean and neat. Sadly the phrase means something horribly different. The phrase was first used during the violent breakup of the former country of Yugoslavia in the early 1990s. Serbs, Croats, and Bosniaks fought in a multisided civil war that featured many horrible atrocities. Journalists from Yugoslavia were the first to use the term *ethnic cleansing* during the early war years. Quickly, the international media picked up the term and began to use it. The United Nations (UN) defines ethnic cleansing as the deliberate act of making an area ethnically homogeneous. It is done by using force or intimidation to remove persons of another ethnic or religious group from a given area.

Ethnic cleansing involves many unsavory practices. In addition to systematic illegal removal, a group can even be annihilated. Extermination is only one despicable practice included in ethnic cleansing. Torture, concentration camps, rape, and other gross violations of human rights are often used to forcefully remove people from their homes and communities. Perpetrators of ethnic cleansing are guilty of crimes against humanity.

The term has now been applied to other situations in many lands including Iraq, the Congo, Sudan, and the Republic of Georgia. Had the term been used during World War II, it would have applied to Adolf Hitler's heinous Holocaust activities. Ethnic cleansing is considered to be a crime against humanity.

Every person on the planet deserves basic human rights, yet many incidences of human "wrongs" persist. Above, Afghan journalism student Sayed Parwez Kambakhsh serves a 20-year sentence for blasphemy. Originally sentenced to death for distributing an article questioning the rights of Muslim women, Kambakhsh was denied legal representation and the opportunity to speak in his own defense. Many believe his sentence is an attempt to intimidate the media.

(formerly Burma) and North Korea are held in a tight dictatorial grip that exemplifies the unfairness of the rule of man.

Fairness and justice dictate that all people are created equal. Thus, human rights should logically apply to all people, regardless of their race, color, gender, creed, sexual orientation, religion, economic status, or any other condition. People are people. They all should possess certain human rights according to international and national documents. Children and youth are guaranteed these rights, as are the aged. Everyone has rights. But are they protected?

In this book we will closely examine the history of human rights. Basic questions will be answered, including:

- What are human rights?
- Where do human rights come from?
- What is the history of human rights?
- What has been the impact of human rights on aboriginal people?
- What has been the impact of human rights on women?
- What has been the impact of human rights on other minorities?
- What human rights issues are facing people today?
- What does the future hold for human rights?

MAKING C⊕NNECTI⊕NS

WHY ARE HUMAN RIGHTS IMPORTANT?

The issue of human rights is gaining more attention in societies around the world. Before our reading journey travels farther, consider the following tasks and write your ideas on a piece of paper.

1 What rights and freedoms do you believe should be human rights for all people?
2 List situations that you believe are human rights issues at the local, national, and global levels.
3 Do you believe human rights are important to you, your family, and your friends? Why?

Place your answers in a safe place, perhaps in this book. Later you can refer back to your early thinking about human rights to see if and how your thinking has changed.

Our discoveries in the journey though human rights will not always be attractive. Far too many wrongs have been committed. But new efforts are also being made to improve human rights around the world. Our path in this book will help you see these efforts and understand how you can help to protect the rights of yourself and others.

As you can already see, this book isn't about just places (geography) or points in time (history). These are only pieces of the puzzle that create a comprehensive picture of the nature and importance of human rights. Other social sciences, such as political science, economics, sociology, and psychology, also contribute very important pieces of the puzzle. The social sciences offer the best guidance in helping us better understand what the human rights puzzle picture looks like. They contribute many powerful ideas that are the point of this book.

Have you figured out what the number 150 million stands for? Tragically, it is the number of people who died from genocide during the twentieth century. In one century, a number equal to almost half the population of the United States was needlessly slain by ruthless tyrants. These crimes violated the most basic human right—the right to life.

WHAT ARE
HUMAN RIGHTS?

Human rights are as basic as human existence. Identifying these rights, however, has been a major quest for humankind for centuries. We know that human rights are defined as the rights and freedoms that all people are entitled to simply because they are human. But what are these rights and freedoms to which we are all entitled? Are there different types of rights and freedoms? Of course! But often they have overlapping characteristics. This chapter digs deeper into the different areas that are identified as human rights.

NATURAL HUMAN RIGHTS

Philosophers have discussed the idea of natural rights since the time of the ancient Greeks, more than 2,000 years ago. They believed that human rights were given either by nature or by God and were a gift to all people at birth. They further believed that these rights could not be taken away.

Thomas Hobbes (1588–1679) was a British philosopher who wrote a book called *Leviathan*. In this book, he imagined a world without government where people would be free to do whatever they wanted. He believed that this would be an evil world filled with conflict and war because anyone could take anything from anybody else. Thus, this hostile world would require a government with the authority to control conflicts. He also contended that any legal rights would then come from government, since the government was providing security. A quote by former U.S. president James Madison reflects the view of Hobbes's thinking: "If men were angels, no government would be necessary."

In contrast to Hobbes, John Locke was a strong advocate for natural rights in the seventeenth century. He believed that people were born into a natural existence, before politics and government. Thus, they were born free, equal, happy, rational, and tolerant. In this state, Locke believed, all people were entitled to life, liberty, and property. These rights were natural and could not be taken or given away.

Locke argued that the role of government was to protect the rights of people in a social contract. A social contract is an agreement between a government and the governed, or citizens. It defines and limits the rights of both parties. Locke believed that if a government failed to protect the rights of the people, the people had a right to revolt and change governments. This is one of many ideas that found its way into the United States' Declaration of Independence. Look for this idea and others of Locke's in the passage below:

> We hold these Truths to be self-evident, that <u>all Men are created equal</u>, that they are <u>endowed by their creator with certain unalienable Rights</u>, that among these are <u>Life, Liberty, and the Pursuit of Happiness</u>. That <u>to secure these Rights, Governments are instituted</u> among Men, <u>deriving their just Powers from the Consent of the Governed</u>, that <u>whenever any</u>

Form of Government becomes destructive of these Ends, it is the Right of the People to alter or to abolish it, and to institute new Government, laying its Foundation on such Principles, and organizing its Powers in such Form, as to them shall seem most likely to effect their Safety and Happiness.

The underlined passages in the Declaration of Independence clearly can be linked to the thinking of Locke and even the ancient Greeks. Thus, the old idea of natural rights is one that is still of key importance in the twenty-first century.

POLITICAL HUMAN RIGHTS

In the social contract between citizens and their government, it is very common to protect political freedoms. These include such rights as freedom of expression, the press, assembly, religion, and the right to life and liberty. These political protections also safeguard citizens and their right to be free from unreasonable searches, arbitrary arrests, torture, cruel and unusual punishment, unfair trials, and *ex post facto* laws. An *ex post facto* law is a situation in which an individual does something that is not against the law, but a law is later passed making the act illegal. Thus, there was no law against the act at the time it was committed, thereby making it an *ex post facto* law. Finally, to be considered innocent of a crime until proven guilty is also a political right. All of these preceding political rights protect citizens from overreaching governments. What does each of these mean?

Freedom of Expression

The freedom of expression is often stated as freedom of speech. However, it can include a number of other ideas, such as freedom of religion. Another example could be artists who express their thoughts in a painting, or poets through their poems. Musicians express their ideas in music, which can also offer political expression. Newspaper editors and political cartoonists may express their ideas in newspapers, just as bloggers are free to put their thoughts into their blogs. The information may not be true, but freedom of expression allows these thoughts to be freely expressed.

JOHN LOCKE ON HUMAN RIGHTS

John Locke was a British philosopher born in 1632. He was born to a tanner's daughter named Agnes Keene, who died when he was an infant. His father, also named John Locke, was a country lawyer. The younger Locke was very bright and received an excellent education as a youth. Later, he continued his education at Oxford, where he became an academic and a medical researcher. He was unsatisfied with much of what he was taught at Oxford and proceeded to develop his own philosophy. Among his books was the *Two Treatises of Government,* published in 1690. The second Treatise is where Locke speaks of the state of nature and natural rights.

Although Locke's *Two Treatises* did not receive wide attention upon publication, it influenced many of the most important political documents existing today. In addition to natural rights, Locke presented powerful political ideas. These included the rule of law, limited government, and the social contract. His thinking has left a wake of political influence on many key documents. Among these are the U.S. Constitution, the Declaration of Independence, Canada's Constitution Act (1867), Australia's constitution (1901), Poland's constitution, the Universal Declaration of Human Rights (UDHR), and many others.

Friends and visitors flocked to see Locke in his last years. He had suffered years of failing and fragile health, but he remained cheerful and wrote into his last month of life. Locke died in 1704 at Oates, Essex (England), at the age of 72. He was buried in a wooden box at a humble grave site on the sunny side of the High Laver Church in Essex. Although Locke's death was humble, his mark upon the world has been lasting.

Limits to the freedom of expression may apply in cases of libel or slander, in which the information is harmful and may hurt the reputation of another. Other limits may also apply, as some information or pictures may not be deemed appropriate by a society. Freedom of expression also includes the right to assemble with others who carry similar beliefs. Thus, protest marches, demonstrations, and other public political activities are included in the freedom of expression. Again, limits are imposed when public safety or the common good of a society are threatened.

Justice

Citizens also have political rights that protect them if they are charged with a crime. The United Nations Human Rights Council (UNHRC) considers all people to be innocent until proven guilty in a public trial. Justice is an important right that can be divided into three forms for better understanding. Each form includes vitally important political rights.

The Center for Civic Education, based in Calabasas, California, has identified three areas of justice. These are distributive justice, procedural justice, and corrective justice. Each of these areas contains rights that are protected by the Universal Declaration of Human Rights (UDHR). For example, Article 9 of this document states, "No one shall be subjected to arbitrary arrest, detention or exile." This means that arrests must be conducted by a process that is fair to the accused person. This is an example of procedural justice. Procedural justice means that there is a fair process conducted.

Article 7 of the UDHR provides an example of distributive justice, which means that justice is fairly distributed to all people. The UDHR states, "All are equal before the law and are entitled without any discrimination to equal protection of the law." Thus, Article 7 provides a clear example of distributive justice. Corrective justice refers to providing punishment in a fair manner. Article 5 clearly reflects corrective justice by stating, "No one shall be subjected to torture or to cruel, inhuman or degrading treatment or punishment."

Other Political Rights

Political human rights allow a citizen to actively and fairly participate as a member of society without undue restrictions by the government. Many rights are severely limited in different societies—especially nondemocratic societies. However, even democratic societies do not always adhere to the UDHR. The United States, for example, has been subject to criticism at home and abroad for perceived human rights violations. Circumstances of prisoners held at Abu Ghraib in Iraq and at Guantanamo Bay Detention Camp in Cuba, for example, have gained international attention because of possible human rights violations. Political rights are vitally important to democratic governments where the people rule. If political opponents or an oppressive government tread on these rights, the society will fail as a democracy.

ECONOMIC HUMAN RIGHTS

Economic human rights seek to protect the ways that people manage their financial situation. The Universal Declaration of Human Rights protects a number of economic rights in Article 25, which states:

> Everyone has the right to a standard of living adequate for the health and well-being of himself and of his family, including food, clothing, housing and medical care and necessary social services, and the right to security in the event of unemployment, sickness, disability, widowhood, old age or other lack of livelihood in circumstances beyond his control.

This statement means that all people have the right to economic protections. People still need to be responsible and work, but they have the right to a sufficient standard of living that provides the basic necessities. The article also gives people the right to protection in times of extreme need, such as failing health or old age.

Other economic rights are protected by the UDHR, including the right to work and freely choose employment. The right to equal pay for equal work and the right to join a union are also protected. In addition, workers have a right to rest, leisure, and paid holidays, and no one can be held in slavery. Even the freedom of movement can be interpreted in one sense as an economic right. People should be free to move from place to place in search of employment, even if it is to another country.

MAKING CONNECTIONS

WHICH RIGHTS DO YOU BELIEVE SHOULD BE PROTECTED IN A COUNTRY'S CONSTITUTION?

The Universal Declaration of Human Rights sets forth many human rights that the international community believes are important. Which of these rights do you believe should be included in your nation's constitution? First, list all the rights that you believe are fundamental for all people in your country. You can draw from the rights discussed in this chapter or you can draw from other sources of information. After you have prepared your list, compare it with your country's constitution. Which rights are on your list and in the constitution? Which are not included? For those rights not included, investigate why they are not included in the constitution.

As a citizen in a democracy, you can influence public policy by seeking to protect rights that you believe should be in your constitution or other public policy. In the United States, this can be accomplished by amending the U.S. Constitution. Other ways also exist, as local governments can implement policies protecting additional rights. These changes can be initiated by citizens—like you!

Economic human rights seek to protect the financial well-being of people. These rights, like political rights, affect our daily lives. Failure to protect economic rights results in failed societies where problems that range from famine to corruption and lawlessness are possible results. The impact on individuals can be even worse when the basic daily needs of food, shelter, and clothing cannot be met sufficiently.

SOCIAL AND CULTURAL HUMAN RIGHTS

Social and cultural human rights provide freedoms within a society. This area includes things such as education and culture. For example, the UDHR provides the right to education. Minimally, this would be an elementary education. But most societies

The reputation of the United States came under international debate when photographs showing the abuse and degradation of inmates by U.S. soldiers at Iraq's Abu Ghraib prison were circulated in the press. Above, an inmate at Abu Ghraib stands bent over in his cell in 2003.

require more schooling. The UDHR also states that higher education, like college or a technical school, should be equally available to everyone and based on merit.

The right to participate in cultural life is also protected by
the UDHR. This means that people can freely participate in
their own culture and the culture of others. The right to share
in scientific advances is also included. The importance of this
right is illustrated by the rapid communications advance for
societies with cell phones. Poor countries that lack costly tele-
phone line infrastructure have leaped a generation with cell
phone technology. Thus, the cultural right to access scientific
advances has allowed millions of people to also advance themselves economically.

Many of the economic, social, and cultural rights contained
in the UDHR are expanded upon in the International Covenant
on Economic, Social and Cultural Rights (ICESCR). This document is a UN treaty adopted in 1966 and implemented in 1976.
Nearly 160 countries have signed this treaty and have committed
themselves to working toward the rights provided in the UDHR.
Canada, Mexico, and Cuba have agreed to the treaty, but the
United States has not, a situation that will be explained further
in Chapter 4.

CIVIL RIGHTS

Another commonly used term is *civil rights*. In the United States,
the civil rights movement has had a tremendous historical and
cultural impact. Its significance has involved political, ethnic,
and economic aspects of society. Civil rights are mostly political
and are based upon the notion that all people are created equal.
In the United States, the Thirteenth and Fourteenth amendments
to the Constitution guarantee civil liberties, due process, freedom
from discrimination, and equal protection under the law. In common U.S. usage, the term *civil rights* is often used in reference to

the rights of racial or ethnic minorities. In recent years, however, it has also been applied to other minority issues, including gender and sexual orientation.

Human rights come in many forms and protect many basic freedoms. The rights discussed in this chapter have been placed in a category, but many of them overlap with one or more others. Whether rights come from nature or from man, they exist today in many written forms. These rights represent powerful ideas for humanity. Chapter 3 discusses sources of human rights and where they exist today.

WHERE DO HUMAN RIGHTS COME FROM?

Human rights today are ideas expressed on paper. The ideas can have tremendous strength and influence, but paper is fragile and can be easily ignored or destroyed. Where are human rights expressed today? Actually, they appear in many places, such as the United Nations Universal Declaration of Human Rights (UDHR), other UN declarations, and various religious teachings. They are also in national and state constitutions and in countless laws, regulations, and ordinances.

Organizations like the Association of South East Asian Nations (ASEAN), the North Atlantic Treaty Organization (NATO), and the European Union (EU) have written statements on human rights. The words are everywhere and establish the foundations and sources of human rights. In this chapter, we will examine many of the different sources of human rights. Also, we will investigate the written documents that set the standards for human rights, liberties, and protections.

EARLY SOURCES

As long as there have been people, there have been acts that violate other human beings. At the same time, there have always been those who seek to achieve a higher level of human rights. Perhaps it started simply with cave people. If they harmed another individual, they were at greater risk of being harmed themselves: a philosophy of "If you club me, I'll club you!" Simple examples like this sometimes convey complex ideas, such as the Bible's Golden Rule asking followers to "do unto others as they would do unto you."

This biblical statement is actually a complex notion that is reflected by nearly all of the world's faiths and philosophies. The idea is built upon the concept of reciprocity, the belief that a person should do toward others what he or she would hope others would do for him or her. For example, the Islamic faith holds that "No one of you is a believer until he desires for his brother that which he desires for himself." Another teaching of Islam states that "None of you [truly] believes until he wishes for his brother what he wishes for himself." In Buddhism, a similar idea is expressed in "Hurt not others in ways that you yourself would find hurtful." In Hinduism, the expression is "This is the sum of duty: Do not do to others what would cause pain if done to you." Nearly every world religion or philosophy holds an idea similar to the Golden Rule and the idea of reciprocity.

Even with so many religions and philosophies holding the value of reciprocity, many only hold the value for others who share their own faith or belief structure. For example, an individual is a devout member of a church. He believes in the idea of reciprocity, but only for those members of his church who are saved. This limited reciprocity has led individuals to discriminate against the human rights of others in the name of their religion. Contemporary examples are evident all around us. There are Christians who fail to advocate for the human rights of gays and lesbians. There are Muslim terrorists who kill and maim others in their jihad (holy war) against Western societies. Neither the Christian Bible nor the Islamic Qur'an condones these activities. Radical followers of both faiths, however, use religion to support actions that result in serious human rights abuses of others outside of their religion.

CHRISTIANITY AND HUMAN RIGHTS

The Bible is the primary book of faith for Christians. Most Christians believe that human rights are important because people are loved by God, not simply because they are human beings. The term *human rights* does not appear in the Bible, but many of its verses teach ideas that promote and support human rights. The earlier example of the Golden Rule is one of those ideas.

Some faiths, such as Catholicism, list human rights in documents that represent the church's philosophy. Many Christian denominations have statements supportive of human rights. One example is provided in an official paper by the General Board of Church and Society of the United Methodist Church. This document states, in part: "Human dignity is the sum total of all human rights. The violation and denial of human rights to any person, individually or collectively, are an affront to this God-given dignity." The World Council of Churches says that Christians must learn about and stand up for human rights. Thus, Christianity is one religious source of human rights with the Bible as its foundation.

ISLAM AND HUMAN RIGHTS

The Qur'an is Islam's Book of Revelation. Muslims believe that the Qur'an is Allah's (God's) word transmitted through the angel Gabriel to the Prophet Muhammad. The Qur'an upholds the value for human life and also values the rights to life, justice, freedom, work, sustenance, privacy, and others. The Qur'an also elevates women in a way that is not often recognized in the real world by some countries with large Muslim populations. According to the Qur'an, women should enjoy all of the general rights and deserve special attention because they are historically disadvantaged.

Similar to Christianity, many within Islam violate basic ideas of their faith when it is convenient politically or when it helps to maintain the religious dominance of men. An example is reflected in a statement by Ayatollah Khomeini of Iran, who said, "What they call human rights is nothing but a collection of corrupt rules worked out by the Zionists to destroy all true religions." By his view, human rights are a Jewish conspiracy even though the Qur'an doesn't reflect this viewpoint. Islamic extremists often

Afghan women browse through a selection of books at a UN-sponsored Women's Day fair in Kabul. Afghanistan is an example of a country that has violated rights of women. Although the holy text of the Qur'an promotes rights for women, these words are misused and violated by many Muslims.

paint the Universal Declaration of Human Rights as a statement influenced by Western countries, rather than a document that reflects universal values. However, the Qur'an, like the Bible, provides key underpinnings for human rights.

JUDAISM AND HUMAN RIGHTS

Basic human rights can be found in the Hebrew Bible (and in the Christian Bible's Old Testament) with the Ten Commandments. A clear example is "You shall not murder." But Jews have gone further in recent decades with a Declaration of Human Rights that was adopted in Montreal, Canada, in 1974. The document's opening statement clearly addresses this by saying, "Human rights are an integral part of the faith and tradition of Judaism. The beliefs that man was created in the divine image, that the human family is one, and that every person is obliged to deal justly with every other person are basic sources of the Jewish commitment to human rights."

Jewish history is filled with followers of the faith suffering human rights abuses, including mass murder. In the twentieth century, the Holocaust saw millions of Jews killed by the Nazis in Europe. These horrifying experiences have caused most Jews to become strong advocates of human rights. Despite overwhelming evidence to the contrary, there are Holocaust deniers. They spread the lie that the Holocaust, and millions of resulting murders, never took place. These Holocaust deniers and people like the late Ayatollah Khomeini seek to deny fundamental human rights to others. Sadly, history is full of such people and deeds. This area will be explored more in Chapter 4.

HINDUISM AND HUMAN RIGHTS

Hinduism is the primary religion in India and is also practiced in other countries around the world. When people think of India, the rigid caste (class) system with foundations in

Hinduism may come to mind. In this system, lower castes are kept in their place by Hindu beliefs that seem very contrary to human rights. Hinduism speaks less of human rights than other religions, even though many Hindus are very serious about preserving human rights. This issue presents a new challenge for Hindus who today are searching through their holy documents, called the Vedas, for guidance on human rights. Versions of the Golden Rule are readily available in Hinduism, with the following two most relevant: "One should not behave toward others in a way which is disagreeable to oneself" and "This is the sum of duty: Do naught unto others which would cause you pain if done to you."

Inconsistencies continue to exist in India between basic human rights, the caste system, and the role of women. Yet, many Indian leaders, including Mohandas K. Gandhi, were strong advocates for human rights and actually had their own human rights violated on many occasions. India's government has also been active in working to reduce the caste system and discrimination against the untouchables, also called Dalits, and women. (In 1947, when India became free of British rule, the caste system was outlawed. The fact that it is still widely practiced more than half a century later is an example of how difficult it is to legislate human tolerance and behavior.)

BUDDHISM AND HUMAN RIGHTS

Buddhist primary documents, like virtually all other major ancient philosophies and religions, do not specifically focus on human rights. This is because the primary holy documents of world religions predate the Western idea of rights and the usage of the term *human rights*. Nevertheless, Buddhism considers all human beings equal. This premise provides a basic foundation for human rights. Basic beliefs include the following guidelines, which are very similar to those expressed by the Golden Rule: ". . . a state that is not pleasing or delightful to me, how could I inflict that upon another?" and "Hurt not others in ways that you yourself would find hurtful."

The fourteenth Dalai Lama has also spoken clearly about human rights by saying, "Peace can only last where human rights are respected, where the people are fed, and where individuals and nations are free." He expanded on human rights by saying:

> All human beings, whatever their cultural or historical background, suffer when they are intimidated, imprisoned or tortured. . . . We must, therefore, insist on a global consensus, not only on the need to respect human rights worldwide, but also on the definition of these rights . . . for it is the inherent nature of all human beings to yearn for freedom, equality and dignity, and they have an equal right to achieve that.

As a religious figure, the Dalai Lama is notable in another respect. He has spoken out against violence toward lesbians and gays. Clearly, he believes that *all* human beings should have their human rights respected.

RELIGIONS, PHILOSOPHIES, AND HUMAN RIGHTS

The idea of reciprocity is common to most of the world's major religions and philosophies. Earlier examples provided a look at Christian, Muslim, Hindu, Jewish, and Buddhist beliefs that relate to the idea of reciprocity. This ancient and well-tested idea provides an essential foundation for human rights.

During recent decades, world conferences held by major religions have stressed the need to protect human rights. This makes great sense because many of their followers have been persecuted because of their beliefs. Buddhists have been persecuted in Myanmar (Burma) and China. Christians have been persecuted and discriminated against in Northern Ireland, China, India, and areas of the Middle East. Muslims have been victims of hate crimes and persecution in the United States, Middle East, and Europe. Jews have been persecuted by Nazis in Germany and in many other countries, including those in the Middle East. Seeing these problems, many international faith gatherings focus upon protecting the rights of all people across the world. The following quote by Pastor Martin Niemöller demonstrates why this is important:

> In Germany they first came for the Communists, and I didn't speak up because I wasn't a Communist.
>
> Then they came for the Jews, and I didn't speak up because I wasn't a Jew.
>
> Then they came for the trade unionists, and I didn't speak up because I wasn't a trade unionist.
>
> Then they came for the Catholics, and I didn't speak up because I was a Protestant.
>
> Then they came for me—and by that time no one was left to speak up.

With major religions now tackling the issue of human rights, the idea of reciprocity may be expanded. Even Native American spiritual beliefs express a basic value for human rights. Over two centuries ago, Nez Percé chief Joseph believed that "The Earth is the mother of all people and all people should have equal rights upon it." World religions working together to protect human rights can be a powerful force for positive change.

THE UNITED NATIONS UNIVERSAL DECLARATION OF HUMAN RIGHTS

In 1945, on the heels of World War II, representatives of many countries met in San Francisco, California, to hammer out details of a new worldwide organization. In October of that year, representatives of 51 countries signed a charter that launched the

United Nations (UN). Three years later, on December 10, 1948, the UN General Assembly adopted the Universal Declaration of Human Rights (UDHR). The vote was 48–0, with eight nations abstaining. These eight included East European satellite states under the Soviet Union's control, South Africa, and Saudi Arabia. Today, UN Day is celebrated on October 24, the organization's anniversary.

Provisions of the UDHR

The *Guinness Book of World Records* lists the UDHR as the world's most translated document. The declaration has 30 articles that touch on a variety of human rights. The articles apply to all people in all countries regardless of any characteristic "such as race, color, sex, language, religion, political or other opinion, national or social origin, property, birth or other status." Selected rights include the following:

- Everyone has the right to life, liberty, and security of person.
- No one can be held as a slave, and slave trade is prohibited.
- No person can be subjected to torture or to cruel, inhuman, or degrading treatment or punishment.
- Everyone is equal under the law and is entitled to protection against discrimination in any form.
- Everyone has a right to have a remedy for any UDHR violations against them by their courts.
- No individual should be subjected to arbitrary arrest, detention, or exile.
- Everyone charged with a crime should be considered innocent until proven guilty.
- Everyone is entitled to a fair and public hearing (trial) with an independent and impartial tribunal (jury).
- No one can be charged for an act that wasn't a crime when the act was committed (*ex post facto* laws).

- Everyone has the right to privacy, family, home, and correspondence.
- Everyone has the freedom of movement within their country and the freedom to leave and return to their country.
- Everyone who is persecuted has the right to leave their country and seek asylum (protection) elsewhere.

This 1955 photo shows a printed document of the Universal Declaration of Human Rights, one of the first documents published by the United Nations. The extensive declaration has 30 articles that address a variety of human rights.

- Everyone has the right to have a nationality.
- Freely consenting adult men and women have the right to marry and form a family—both are entitled to equal rights in the marriage and also in any divorce if it should happen.
- Everyone has the right to own property, and it cannot be taken away arbitrarily.
- Everyone has the right to freedom of thought, conscience, and religion—this includes the right to change religion if an individual wants to.
- Everyone has the freedom of opinion and expression.
- Everyone has the right to freedom of peaceful assembly (gathering) and association—this also includes the right to not be forced into joining.
- Everyone has the right to take part in his or her government, either directly or through freely chosen representatives.
- Everyone has the right to work, to free choice of employment, to good working conditions, to join unions, to fair compensation, and to equal pay without discrimination on any basis.
- Everyone has the right to rest and leisure with reasonable working hours and paid holidays.
- Everyone has the right to a standard of living adequate for the health and well-being of himself and of his family.
- Everyone has a right to an education that is free at the early levels and that promotes understanding, tolerance, human rights, and friendship among all nations, religions, and races.
- Everyone has the right to freely participate in the cultural life of the community.

The preceding list includes many important provisions from the UDHR. Check the Internet for the full UDHR document.

INTERNATIONAL COVENANT ON ECONOMIC, SOCIAL AND CULTURAL RIGHTS

The United Nations has continued in its quest to extend and protect human rights beyond the original UDHR. In 1966, the body adopted a treaty called the International Covenant on Economic, Social and Cultural Rights (ICESCR). This document was implemented in 1976 and had been signed by 157 parties as of 2009. Notable among the nonsigners is the United States. U.S. representatives signed the document in 1966, but presidents Richard Nixon and Gerald Ford refused to sign the treaty. President Jimmy Carter did sign the treaty, but he was not able to get the two-thirds vote of the U.S. Senate needed for its ratification (passing). Since that time, President Ronald Reagan, President George H.W. Bush, and President George W. Bush have all opposed the treaty. President Bill Clinton favored ICESCR, but he didn't pursue it because the opposition party controlled the U.S. Senate.

The ICESCR document commits the countries that have signed it to providing economic, social, and cultural rights. These include the rights to work, to social security, to family life (including the protection of children), to health, to an adequate standard of living, to education, and to participate in cultural life. Opposition by some U.S. presidents was based on the belief that these rights should be social goals, rather than rights protected by law.

INTERNATIONAL COVENANT ON CIVIL AND POLITICAL RIGHTS

Another UN document called the International Covenant on Civil and Political Rights (ICCPR) was developed in 1966 and implemented in 1976. It is not a coincidence that ICESCR and ICCPR have the same dates. This is because both were originally in one document. Some countries would sign on to one part but not the other. Therefore, it was split into two parts. The United States was one of the hesitant countries. It signed and ratified ICCPR with some reservations, but, as described earlier, it did not sign ICESCR. Even as a signer of ICCPR, the United States has been criticized internationally for failing to implement some portions of the document.

ICCPR seeks to protect the political and civil rights of all individuals. Specific rights include protection against torture, execution, and arbitrary arrest. Other rights include aspects of

ORGANIZATIONS WORKING TO PROTECT HUMAN RIGHTS

Governments and religions aren't the only ones concerned about protecting human rights. Some nongovernmental organizations (NGOs) have proven to be very effective in protecting them. Some of these organizations, such as Amnesty International, Freedom House, Human Rights Watch, and Physicians for Human Rights, are global in their scope. Other organizations are regional or nationwide. One example is the American Civil Liberties Union (ACLU), which operates in the United States. It has the specific purpose of defending and extending individual freedoms guaranteed by the U.S. Bill of Rights.

Some local human rights NGOs may be affiliates of national or international organizations such as Amnesty International or the ACLU. Others may be "homegrown" and have arisen because of local concerns or needs. These include NGOs such as the Ella Baker Center for Human Rights in San Francisco or the Aboriginal Rights Coalition in Australia. The power of NGOs working in human rights cannot be underestimated. For example, in 2008 there were widespread protests of the Olympic flame in support of a free Tibet. The protesters gained widespread Internet attention and front-page coverage in newspapers around the world. Because of the work of NGOs and individuals, China agreed to meet with the Dalai Lama to discuss the denial of human rights in China-controlled Tibet. Most NGOs work behind the scenes in their daily quest to improve the condition of people in their community and around the world.

procedural justice. These include the right to the rule of law, an attorney, and an impartial trial. The rule of law holds the belief that all people, even leaders, must obey laws. In contrast, the rule of man puts an individual, such as the former leader of Cuba, Fidel Castro, above the law. ICCPR holds that the rule of law should prevail. Not surprisingly, Cuba did not sign on to ICCPR until Fidel Castro left power in 2008.

Other provisions of ICCPR protect civil rights and prevent discrimination on the basis of gender, religion, race, and other human differences. The document reaffirms the right of a citizen to participate in political affairs. It also seeks to protect the freedoms of belief including free speech, association, press, and the right to assemble. The right to speak out against a person's government is explicit in the document. ICCPR also has two optional provisions that hold interest in many countries. One is the optional provision that abolishes the death penalty, and the second provides a way for individuals to make complaints against their government.

NATIONAL CONSTITUTIONS

A country's constitution establishes the basic operating system of government, and most constitutions also establish the rights of citizens within a country. In democracies, the constitution serves as the social contract between the people and their government. Most countries hold the constitution as the most important political document that a country possesses. However, in dictatorships the constitution may hold little value, as the leader(s) are above the law and the constitution.

The U.S. Constitution

Human rights and freedoms are usually provided in a country's constitution. For example, in the United States, the Bill of Rights was added to the Constitution to protect the rights of citizens. Many of the ideas are very similar and even identical to those found in the UDHR, which was written a century and a half later. The founders of the United States wanted to provide citizens with basic rights and freedoms. Among these are the freedoms of speech, religion, and press, and the right to assemble. The right to privacy is implied in the Fourth Amendment. The right to a fair trial, due process, and other judicial protections are provided in the Fifth through Eighth amendments. The Ninth Amendment is very interesting in that it states, "The enumeration in the Constitution of certain rights shall not be construed to deny or disparage others retained by the people." This means that other rights and freedoms exist beyond those specifically listed in the Bill of Rights. This also provides a method of limiting a government that could use its power to restrict basic rights that were not listed.

One right that is in the U.S. Bill of Rights, but is not included in the UDHR, is the Second Amendment, which states, "A well regulated militia, being necessary to the security of a free state, the right of the people to keep and bear arms, shall not be infringed." Some believe that this amendment denies human rights to others who are victims of crimes with guns. They believe that it is incongruent with the rights mentioned in the Declaration of Independence, which include life, liberty, and the pursuit of happiness. Others believe that the framers intended exactly the words as they are written in the Second Amendment.

Canada's Charter of Rights and Freedoms

The Canadian Charter of Rights and Freedoms serves as Canada's bill of rights. It is in the first part of Canada's Constitution Act, which was implemented in 1982. In contrast to the United States, many more freedoms are specifically listed and include:

- Freedom of conscience
- Freedom of religion
- Freedom of thought
- Freedom of belief
- Freedom of expression

- Freedom of press
- Freedom of peaceful assembly
- Freedom of association
- The right to vote
- The right to a democratic government
- The right to life, liberty, and security of the person
- The right to judicial and trial protections including equality under the law
- The right to travel outside and within Canada

Other rights are also protected with Canada's constitution, which chooses to list protected rights, rather than is done in the U.S. Constitution with the Ninth Amendment.

MAKING C⊕NNECTI⊕NS

COMPARING YOUR HUMAN RIGHTS

The Universal Declaration of Human Rights is a key document that serves as a litmus test for citizens to use in evaluating their own constitution and rights. How good are the protections you have as a citizen? To compare, first locate the rights and freedoms stated in your national constitution (for U.S. citizens, the Bill of Rights, and for Canadians, the Canadian Charter of Rights and Freedoms). Identify the similarities and differences between the constitutional protections and the UDHR provisions. Make a list of the items that are the same and those that are different. This research can be extended by identifying rights and freedoms guaranteed by other levels of government.

In addition, if you practice a religion or philosophy, identify the human rights positions taken by the institutions with which you identify. How do these institutions stand on the UDHR? What similarities and differences exist? How can they be explained?

Constitutions from Around the World

With access to the Internet, the constitutions of nearly all countries in the world are available. This allows citizens to check not only their own constitution but also those of other countries to compare how human rights and freedoms are protected. Most countries have constitutions that protect human rights. As with all written government documents, the guarantees provided are only as good as the government itself. In democracies, citizens have the responsibility of watching over their government to ensure that constitutional provisions for human rights are protected. In dictatorships, the citizens have little or no power; human rights violations are frequently carried out by the government to maintain power.

The southern African country of Zimbabwe is an example of a nation in which the constitution, as amended in 2005, guarantees many freedoms. Under the constitution, people are granted freedom of expression, conscience, assembly, association, and movement. Yet during the 2008 presidential election, many political opponents were intimidated or even killed for speaking out against the government in power. The government of incumbent president Robert Mugabe also rigged voting, bought votes, and openly harassed and tortured supporters of the opposition. All of the attempts to retain political power caused Mugabe to repeatedly violate the human rights of the citizens of Zimbabwe—even rights protected by the constitution. Thus Zimbabwe's neighbors, the international community, and its own citizens worked to try and protect the people in the country.

REGIONAL AND LOCAL GOVERNMENT PROTECTIONS

The constitutions and charters of many regional and local governments can also provide for the protections of human rights. Regional governments may be called by different names in

It is important for nations to have constitutions that specifically outline human rights for their citizens, but it is even more critical for the governments of these nations to adhere to their constitutions. Above, human rights activists call for the release of Jestina Mukoko, director of the Zimbabwe Peace Project, who was abducted in 2008 by Zimbabwe state security agents under authoritarian president Robert Mugabe. Mukoko was released three months later.

different countries. For example, there are 50 state governments in the United States, but Canada refers to most of its political regions as provinces. Canada's political subdivisions include 10 provinces and 3 territories. The larger subdivisions of a country may be called districts, oblasts, republics, regions, divisions, states, provinces, or other terms. Many of these entities have a constitution or charter that includes rights and freedoms. Some do not. Their national constitution provides the protections by which all citizens must abide. Many regional government documents simply restate the rights and freedoms listed in the national constitution. Others, however, may choose to expand upon these rights.

There are also many local governments, such as communities, counties, parishes, and even school districts. Many other terms are used by countries to describe various units of local government. Once again, rights and freedoms may be protected by local government laws and documents. For example, Duluth, Minnesota, passed resolution 03-0486 in 2003, which listed and affirmed the rights of all people. Many levels of government provide human rights commissions that are charged with the responsibility of protecting human rights within their jurisdiction. Even elected public school boards assist by requiring the teaching of human rights in the curriculum.

COURT PROTECTIONS

Courts can also provide decisions that establish or clarify human rights and freedoms. A case from the United States provides a good example. In 1958, Mildred Jeter married Richard Loving in Washington, D.C. Afterward, they returned to Virginia, where they were charged with violating a state law that prohibited interracial marriages. Mildred was black and Richard was white. A Virginia trial followed and found Richard and Mildred Loving to be guilty and sentenced them to a year in jail. They also were offered the opportunity to leave Virginia for no less than 25 years and thereby avoid the prison term.

The foregoing case, called *Loving v. Virginia*, was later appealed to the U.S. Supreme Court in 1967. The nine Supreme Court justices ruled unanimously that Virginia's law violated the Fourteenth Amendment to the U.S. Constitution, which guarantees due process and equal protection under the law. Thus, court cases are another source that clarifies and protects human rights.

GLOBAL CONNECTIONS

In this chapter, we have examined a variety of sources of human right protections. Some are offered in holy religious documents that are based upon the idea of reciprocity. Others are governmental documents such as constitutions, laws, codes, court decisions, and ordinances that list or clarify specific human rights and freedoms. Still others are provided by international bodies such as the United Nations. Despite all of these protections on paper, human rights violations continue to occur. Chapter 4 examines the history of human rights and some of the terrible "human wrongs" that continue to challenge individuals, countries, and the global community.

WHAT IS THE HISTORY OF HUMAN RIGHTS?

History is scarred by horrendous violations of human rights. The most basic right—the right to life—has brazenly been taken away from people by violent regimes, hate mongers, and other bullies who litter the pages of history. In 2008, thousands of people were murdered in political oppression in societies ranging from Zimbabwe to Iraq. The right to life was also violated in Myanmar (Burma) when a devastating cyclone hit the country in May 2008.

The country's heavy-handed military dictators at first refused to allow international aid to flow freely into the country to help the millions who were starving and homeless. Instead, they chose to let people fester in disease and starvation while the international community waited for the government to allow them to help. More than 100,000 people died or ended up missing because the government was slow to open the doors to international help. The cyclone couldn't have been prevented, but the starvation and disease that followed could have been greatly decreased. This is but one of many tragic examples of how the right to life, liberty, and the pursuit of happiness has been violated through time.

This chapter describes various atrocities that have taken place in violation of human rights. Emphasis is focused upon abuses denying the right to life, liberty, and the pursuit of happiness. Any chapter discussing these horrible actions is incomplete, as history is far too full of them. Thus, selected cases will be described, along with some of the remedies that have been used to address human wrongs.

HUMAN RIGHTS ATROCITIES IN HISTORY

Genocide is a form of ethnic cleansing. The term is used to describe situations in which planned and systematic destruction of a particular group occurs. Victims may be persecuted or even killed because of their ethnicity, race, tribal affiliation, or religious beliefs. The intended purpose of genocide is to extinguish the members of a particular group, even the unborn offspring. Genocide is a gross violation of human rights and specifically the right to life.

Nazi Germany

An extreme example of genocide was committed during World War II by the German Nazi government. The Nazis under Adolf Hitler intended to destroy Jews and many other groups. Also included were Poles, Gypsies (also referred to as Rom), Russians, homosexuals, political dissidents, Christians, and even the disabled. More than 6 million Jews were killed during the Holocaust, as were an additional 5 million non-Jewish victims. The Nazis would systematically steer Jews into gas chambers in their sick efforts to eliminate the religion. Others were herded into concentration camps, like cattle, where they could barely exist. In the end it is estimated that nearly 11 million people were massacred.

Perhaps the best-known and most extreme genocide in modern history was the Holocaust committed by Adolf Hitler's Nazi government. Hitler's dream was an Aryan nation, and he ordered the elimination of millions of human lives in pursuit of that goal. Above, a group of children are liberated from the Auschwitz concentration camp in 1945.

Bosnian War

World War II was not the only time when specific peoples were targeted by others for annihilation. The early 1990s saw a heated division taking place within the former country of Yugoslavia. Serb, Croat, and Bosniak (Bosnian Muslim) groups each sought to become independent and resorted to genocidal efforts to eliminate the other groups. The term *ethnic cleansing* was coined in reference to the removal and genocide of these various groups. The war lasted from 1992 to 1995, when the international community stepped in with NATO and used military action.

The Dayton (Ohio) Peace Agreement was signed in late 1995 and halted the fighting. Atrocities committed during the war included ethnic cleansing, mass rapes, and genocide. An estimated 100,000 people died during the war. Genocide was rampant. For example at Srebrenica, a city in eastern Bosnia-Herzegovina, 8,000 men were slaughtered in 1995. Others fled the country in search of safety. Other atrocities and killings were staged in the Lasva Valley, Prijedor, Zvornik, Banja Luka, and Foca. The initial fragile peace has now stretched into years without war flaring up again. Many of the war criminals have been brought to justice by the international community.

Cambodia's Killing Fields

Cambodia was the site of another horrendous genocide. A political party called the Khmer Rouge took power in 1975 and ended a five-year civil war. The new government immediately embarked on a plan to evacuate the cities and move people into rural areas. Pol Pot, the Khmer Rouge leader, banned almost everything modern, including medicine, schools, stores, banks, and religion. Cambodian society was thrown into chaos as people starved or were killed. Nearly 30 percent of the country's population died or were killed by the barbaric rule of the Khmer Rouge. Hundreds of thousands were buried in mass graves. An estimated 2 million people died needlessly because of the oppressive rule of Pol Pot's regime. *The Killing Fields*, a movie released in 1984, presents a dismal story of this tragic event. In 1979, Cambodia was finally relieved of the Khmer Rouge nightmare when Vietnam invaded and removed Pol Pot's murderous regime.

Soviet Union and China

Communist governments under Joseph Stalin in the Soviet Union and Mao Tse-tung in China also committed genocide on massive scales. Stalin killed more than 5 million Ukrainians during 1932 and 1933 with a forced famine. This widespread starvation was tragically ironic because Ukraine was the breadbasket of the

Soviet Union. Stalin persecuted political enemies and others in his attempt to impose an iron grip on the country. Those who were not immediately killed were shipped to the *gulags* (prison camps) in Siberia (the portion of Russia, or the USSR, lying east of the Ural Mountains), where they disappeared. The millions of deaths caused by Stalin exceed even those of Adolf Hitler, making him the one of the worst murderers of the twentieth century.

The devilish deeds of China's Mao Tse-tung may be even worse than those of Stalin. An estimated 40 million people died during his rule. Many died in the civil war between two political groups, the Communists and the Nationalists. Others died of famine in the 1950s or during the Cultural Revolution in the 1960s. Mao also crushed Tibet in 1959, when the Dalai Lama fled after he had repudiated China's claim to the region. In the wake of the Dalai Lama's departure, hundreds of thousands of Tibetans died. Thousands of children were taken from their families, and an unknown number of people were arrested. Starvation sapped the life out of others who remained in Tibet after nearly a million Tibetans had migrated to India and other parts of the world. Thus, the legacy of Mao is marked by the blood of millions. He and other ruthless dictators created human tragedies that cost 150 million people their right to life during the twentieth century.

Genocide in Earlier Times

Genocide was hardly new in the twentieth century. Even the Bible has references to extermination of peoples. In 2 Chronicles 4:41, for example, there is reference to David's elimination of the Amalekites. The fierce Mongol leader Genghis Khan and his horsemen were ruthless; they killed anyone who stood in their way as they amassed the world's largest empire in the thirteenth century. European arrival in the Americas resulted in the deaths of countless Native Americans. Some of these deaths were unintended. The Europeans introduced diseases that were unknown in the Americas and against which the Native population had no natural immunity. African peoples sold each other into slavery, resulting in an estimated 9 million

SOUTH AFRICA'S APARTHEID PAST

Located at the southern tip of Africa is the country of South Africa. This nation has a checkered past in terms of racial relations. The former white governments segregated the races in the country with a policy called apartheid. The word *apartheid* in the Afrikaans language means "separateness." This policy was advanced by the National Party, which was composed primarily of white Afrikaners of Dutch heritage. The policies instituted a very strict legal separation based on race. Four groups were identified in South Africa: black, white, colored, and Asian. Examples of apartheid laws included such things as:

- A ban on mixed marriages or sex with other races
- A ban on using the same facilities, including restaurants, toilets, and swimming pools
- Identity cards that specified one's race
- Restrictions on movement by the creation of racial group areas and forced removal to these areas
- Taking South African citizenship away from blacks by granting citizenship in their racial group area
- Discrimination in employment based on race
- Separation of races in all education, social events, and athletics

Naturally, blacks and other South African minorities, led by Nelson Mandela, Bishop Desmond Tutu, and others, resisted these policies that violated basic human rights. The international community, led by the United Nations, took a firm stand and isolated the Afrikaans-dominated South African government because of apartheid. After of them being sent to the Americas. Many died in the inhumane process that treated people as property to be bought and sold. African tribes, European slave traders, and plantation

years of internal strife and border wars, the National Party under F.W. de Klerk negotiated the end of apartheid with the black-dominated African National Congress (ANC). The racist policy was totally eliminated in 1994 when the ANC came to power.

Following the end of apartheid, South Africa's black population came into power. They immediately faced a major question: What should the new and true democracy do to address the previous racial wrongdoings imposed by the National Party? The answer to this question was an outcome of the negotiations between the National Party and the ANC. The National Party wanted amnesty for all who had committed crimes during the era of apartheid. Mandela argued that full disclosure of the crimes must precede any amnesty. The resulting compromise created the Truth and Reconciliation Commission (TRC), which was established in 1995 and chaired by Bishop Tutu.

The TRC began hearings in 1996. Both victims and perpetrators of human rights atrocities came forward to present their cases. The commission had the authority to restore the rights and dignity of victims and to give amnesty to those who had committed crimes. This process aided the newly democratic government of South Africa and has helped to heal a nation divided by racism and laws that violated basic human rights. The commission presented its report in late 1998 and found that human rights violations had been committed. These violations were not only by the National Party but also by the ANC, whose liberation forces were guilty of crimes. Most believe that the truth and reconciliation process has provided a bridge to a better and more democratic future where human rights are respected.

owners (as well as others) in the Americas all contributed to the barbaric practice.

The tragic consequences of genocide, slavery, rape, and imprisonment remain in societies around the world. The psychological impact has been monumental. Memories for this repugnant behavior are, as they should be, very long. Although the cases mentioned in this section are unspeakable, they are not the only cases. Millions of others have suffered and died because of ruthless dictatorships and outside invaders. Even the tragic consequences of September 11, 2001, presented a new, modern-day form of genocide perpetrated by Osama bin Laden and his sordid followers. History will stand in judgment of these tyrants and their murderous deeds. But society has also worked to punish those responsible for these human rights atrocities.

ATTEMPTS TO REMEDY HUMAN RIGHTS VIOLATIONS

The situation left after eras of human rights atrocities has presented immense challenges for nations and the global community. Are there to be trials and should justice be given to those who did not provide this right to their victims? Are the perpetrators to be punished, and if so, how? Is giving them the death penalty a human rights violation? What happens to the victims of these atrocities? What about the families of those killed during attempts at genocide? The aftermath of eras of human rights atrocities is a difficult period that can foretell the type of society that will emerge. If, for example, revenge is exacted in the harshest of degrees, does the new society simply fall to the same low moral level as the earlier regime? On the other hand, if those who perpetrated human rights crimes are not severely punished, does it encourage others to commit atrocities?

This topic is important. It is one in which history yields many examples that have failed, some that have partially worked, and others that have been successful. Only a few cases can be

MAKING C⊕NNECTI⊕NS

WHAT HUMAN RIGHTS PROBLEMS OCCURRED IN YOUR NATION'S HISTORY?

Few countries, if any, have clean records in terms of human rights. In the evolution of societies, many groups have their fundamental human rights violated. Those who suffer from violations include men, women, minorities, aboriginal people, children, political opponents, foreign enemies, criminals, and many others. For example, Cherokee Indians in Georgia were forced to move from their lands by the Indian Removal Act of 1830. Some in Congress, like Henry Clay and Daniel Webster, opposed the law, but it passed and was signed by President Andrew Jackson. Thousands of Cherokee were herded like animals to Oklahoma, and more than 4,000 died in what is now called the Trail of Tears.

The litany of human rights violations in a country can take many forms, including prohibitions against voting by segments of the population such as women or minorities. Economic discrimination and denial of equal opportunity have been frequent. So has the persecution of individuals and groups who are politically opposed to the government or the prevailing views of a particular time period. Religious persecution has also been a problem in many countries, along with persecution of homosexuals in countries as diverse as Iran and the United States.

Investigate the history of your country. What human rights violations have taken place? Who has had their rights violated? Have these violations continued, or have they been corrected? What areas of human rights need to be improved today in your society? What steps might be taken to correct existing violations and improve conditions for those involved?

examined on these pages. But they are instructive in terms of the paths that have been taken after mass human rights violations. However, a sad fact of history remains that many of the worst of the world's villains were not held accountable for their crimes against humanity. Stalin, Mao Tse-tung, and Hitler, for example, escaped punishment by dying first. Hitler died by his own hand before being captured by Allied forces at the end of World War II.

International Tribunals After World War II

Although Hitler escaped formal punishment, many of his Nazi associates did not. In response to the human rights atrocities committed during the war, many members of the major Axis nations (Nazi Germany, Imperial Japan, and Fascist Italy) were subjected to trials. The most famous of these were the Nuremberg Trials held in Germany.

A military tribunal was established by the London Agreement, which was signed by the United States, the Soviet Union, and the United Kingdom. Each of these three countries had a judge and alternate judge appointed to the tribunal. The tribunal was given the task of trying people who were charged with war crimes and crimes against humanity. Nazi leaders and key supporters were tried. As a result of deliberations, 12 were sentenced to death by hanging and 7 others were sentenced to 10 years to life in prison. More than 100 other Nazis were convicted and sentenced in later trials.

Similar trials were held in Tokyo, Japan, after the war in the Pacific had ended. Even though they were less publicized internationally, 26 Japanese leaders were sentenced to death or life imprisonment. Hideki Tojo was one of these. He was a general in the Imperial Japanese army and prime minister of Japan during World War II. Tojo testified that the emperor ordered him to carry out his atrocities in China, Korea, the Philippines, and other areas of Southeast Asia. Despite his testimony, he was convicted and hanged, whereas the emperor was never prosecuted. Hirohito, the emperor, was not tried, as the Allies believed that the war with Japan would have gone on much longer if he had been subjected to prosecution. Thus, Emperor Hirohito lived until 1989 without his role being clarified by a trial.

Former Yugoslav president Slobodan Milošević stood trial for genocide and other war crimes, but he died before a verdict was delivered. In the midst of the war in the Balkans, the UN launched an investigation into the human rights abuses that were occurring in the conflict. It was decided that these atrocities could be classified as war crimes and should be prosecuted.

Balkan War Crimes Trials

Following the breakup of Yugoslavia, the international community again held war crimes trials. This time the setting was The Hague in the Netherlands, where the United Nations established the International Criminal Tribunal for the former Yugoslavia (ICTY). This tribunal was the first to conduct a trial with a head of state, Serbia's Slobodan Milošević, as a defendant. Others were also prosecuted for war crimes and crimes against humanity. Serbia was reluctant to turn Milošević over to the tribunal, but the country finally did in 2001. However, Milošević died in 2006 before his trial was completed. Others, like Bosnian Serb general

Radislav Krstic, were found guilty of genocide for massacring thousands of Bosniak men at Srebrenica in 1995. Some accused war criminals still remain at large, much to the dissatisfaction of people in the Balkans.

Tribunals in Africa

Tribunals have been set up in Africa after decades of horrible atrocities and human rights violations. Among these are Rwanda in 1996 and Sierra Leone in 2003. Hundreds of thousands of people died in the civil wars in these two countries during the 1990s. The shocking situation in Rwanda was well told in the popular and powerful 2004 movie *Hotel Rwanda*, which starred Don Cheadle. The increasing use of international tribunals to administer justice to people, including leaders, who have perpetrated human rights atrocities is viewed as a positive step forward. Although problems still exist in administering international law, these early steps may help to hold leaders and other people responsible for their actions.

Another approach was put forth in South Africa with a process called Truth and Reconciliation. This process has shown merit in helping a nation to transform itself from an era of human rights violations and atrocities to a democratic society where the rule of law prevails. This approach has been successfully replicated in other areas, such as Morocco, since the original effort in South Africa.

GLOBAL CONNECTIONS

In this chapter, we have examined appalling examples of human rights violations. The most basic right, the right to life, has systematically been taken from millions of people. In some trouble spots, it continues to be a major problem even today. Genocide and murder continue to rob people around the world of their lives. However, steps have been taken to address these situations by holding perpetrators accountable. Two important steps have been taken since World War II. These include the international tribunals that seek to bring the masterminds of crimes against humanity to justice, and the Truth and Reconciliation process. Hopefully, these and other processes will discourage dictators, despots, and deranged governments from violating the human rights of their citizens.

Other rights, besides the right to life, have also been unwillingly forfeited by people throughout history. These include political, economic, social, and legal rights that will be discussed more in Chapters 5, 6, and 7. History is loaded with the stories of oppressed people who have been subjugated unfairly by their governments and others. Chapter 5 examines how aboriginal people have been treated by foreigners, their government, and ruling majorities.

HUMAN RIGHTS OF ABORIGINAL PEOPLE

Aboriginal people were the first to settle and occupy a land area. Many of these cultures are ancient, with a history that dates back thousands of years. As a result, the people treasured their land and the culture that they developed over the centuries. Their culture and lifestyle reflected their use of the environment and the land they occupied. Their culture included such things as a language, an economic system, a set of beliefs, and a system of justice. As the first permanent occupants of their lands, it could be assumed that the lands were theirs. This, however, is an assumption that has proven wrong many times in history. The names of these groups are many. They include the diverse Native American groups, Australia's Aborigines, New Zealand's Maori, Finland's Sami people, the Ainu of northern Japan, and others scattered around the planet.

These indigenous groups existed before outsiders arrived in their lands. New arrivals often came armed with superior technology. They had more effective weapons and means of transportation. They also arrived carrying diseases against which aboriginal people had no natural resistance. First contacts were explorations that later turned to trade. Soon, European nations such as England, France, Spain, Portugal, and the Netherlands were in a race to build colonial empires. They accomplished this goal by seizing political control of new lands. The "new" lands, however, were already home to indigenous people and, in places such as Africa and Asia, huge established populations. Wars were fought, old cultural elements were lost, and new culture traits were gained from the colonial masters. Intermarriages were common. By today's standards, however, human rights violations were rampant. Modern countries have sought ways to make up for the past sins of governments, overzealous churches, and businesses.

This chapter explores some of the human rights issues that have confronted aboriginal peoples and how these have been addressed. Numerous problems still exist. Many aboriginal people face human rights situations that are different from those of more contemporary cultures.

SOCIAL AND CULTURAL HUMAN RIGHTS OF ABORIGINAL PEOPLE

Aboriginal cultures are a treasure that humankind is rapidly losing. In an era of rapid mass transportation and communication, many indigenous cultures are losing their identity. They are being absorbed into the surrounding dominant culture at an alarming rate. Some people are unconcerned about the loss. Today, however, it is widely recognized that aboriginal cultures possess boundless information, much of which is useful to the outside world. Many modern medicines have been adopted from aboriginal cultures. So have nearly all of our food staples. Folk music, art, and dance are very popular today. Archery, kayaks, and the boomerang were all borrowed from traditional societies. So are many words in our language.

One example of the value of Native American language in the United States was the use of code based on the Navajo language during World War II. These Navajo were bilingual. They used their coded native language to baffle the Japanese, who were trying to steal American secrets during the war in the Pacific region. Navajo code talkers were also used during the Korean War. Little known is that other aboriginal languages were also used for the same purposes earlier in history. These included languages of the Cherokee, Choctaw, and Comanche, and even the Basques from Spain.

The rights of aboriginal societies are enumerated in the Universal Declaration of Human Rights. These include social and cultural rights that are vitally important to indigenous peoples. They want the right to practice their own culture and rights to the lands that they have claimed historically. Basically, what they most want is the right to maintain their own separate identity.

The Quest for Human Rights

Indigenous people have approached the international community with grievances since the 1920s, when American Indians reached out to the League of Nations. This was repeated after the United Nations was created. Early efforts were unsuccessful, even though they generated media attention. The United Nations became more involved in the 1970s as issues such as discrimination and slavery gained greater attention. A major UN study was conducted, with the results released in the early 1980s. This study identified a number of human rights issues facing aboriginal peoples. The UN also suggested remedies in the areas of housing, land, health, and culture, including language, education, and religious practices. In 1982, the UN established the Working Group on Indigenous Populations. This group focused its attention on the special condition held by aboriginal people as compared to other minorities.

The UN Working Group has had two primary responsibilities. The first is "to review national developments pertaining to the promotion and protection of the human rights and fundamental freedoms of indigenous peoples." The second is "to develop international standards concerning the rights of indigenous peoples, taking account of both the similarities and the differences in their situations and aspirations throughout the world." The Working Group continued its efforts by drafting the UN Declaration on the Rights of Indigenous Peoples (UNDRIP). After decades of work, the resolution was adopted by the UN General Assembly in 2007 by a vote of 144 to 4, with 11 countries abstaining.

Rights Contained in the UNDRIP

Some of the social and cultural rights given to indigenous people by this document include:

- All the rights provided in the Universal Declaration of Human Rights
- The right to be free from discrimination because of their aboriginal status
- The right to self-determination
- The right to maintain and strengthen their social and cultural institutions
- The right to a nationality
- The right to not be subjected to forced assimilation or destruction of their culture
- The right to not have their children taken by force
- The right to mechanisms that protect them from losing their lands, cultural values, or ethnic identities
- The right to not be forced into assimilation or integration
- The right to belong to an indigenous community or nation
- The right to practice and revitalize their religious, spiritual, and cultural traditions and customs
- The right to not be removed from their lands
- The right to control their own educational systems

While most countries voted in favor of the UNDRIP, four did not. These included countries with significant aboriginal populations: the United States, Canada, Australia, and New Zealand. Why would these progressive nations oppose this human rights agreement for indigenous people? Their concerns mainly included the sections on self-determination, land claims, and resource rights. Thus, the sections of UNDRIP that pertain to social and cultural rights for aboriginal people appear to be supported by these four countries. Some of the economic and political issues, however, have not yet been resolved.

With the UNDRIP, the international community has voted to protect essential rights of aboriginal peoples. This will allow them to better preserve their culture and social traditions. The wrongs of the past are too numerous to discuss, but, if the international community holds to its stated values, the status of indigenous people should improve. This means that they should now be able to freely practice and preserve their way of life in ways not provided before 2007. As with all rights, battles will be fought to protect and preserve what the UN has stated and adopted.

INDIGENOUS PEOPLE AND POLITICAL RIGHTS

The political rights of indigenous people have also been precarious. For example, in the United States, Native Americans did not even become citizens until 1924, with the passage of the Indian Citizenship Act (Snyder Act). This act allowed Native Americans to vote in federal elections. But it was not until 1957 that the last state, Utah, allowed them to vote.

In Australia, Aborigines and other "non-whites" were banned from voting by the 1902 Franchise Act. It was not until 1962 that the country's aboriginal population gained the legal right to vote in federal elections. Full citizenship rights for Aborigines were not guaranteed until 1967.

An Aboriginal family stand outside their home in Sydney, Australia. The country's history of mistreatment of indigenous people, including removal of children from their families, has had lasting effects. Aborigines—one of Australia's indigenous groups—die at a much faster rate than the rest of the population, and life expectancy is markedly shorter.

Political rights extend beyond just voting and include legal and political protections that are also addressed in the UDHR and UNDRIP. Among these rights are those designed to provide for equal protection under the law. These include the right to a free and fair trial, representation in trials, protections against arbitrary arrest, freedom of expression and movement, and the political freedoms discussed in previous chapters.

Native American Governments

Some aboriginal people, such as many Native Americans in the United States, have their own political structures. This self-governance recognizes their special situations and allows people self-determination on political matters. For some, this takes the form of tribal governments, such as the Rosebud Sioux Tribe in South Dakota. The Tribal Council operates under the Rosebud Sioux Tribal Constitution, which also contains a Bill of Rights. Included in these rights are essential political rights such as

AUSTRALIA'S NATIONAL "SORRY DAY"

On February 13, 2008, Australia's prime minister Kevin Rudd went on national television to apologize to the country's Aboriginal and Torres Strait Islander populations. Newspapers covered the event with massive front-page stories, and people talked about the event on the streets of the bustling city of Sydney and the dusty outback roads by Alice Springs. Why was the prime minister apologizing? What had happened?

For nearly 100 years, the Australian government had a policy of removing Aboriginal and Torres Strait Islander children from their homes. At the time, the government believed that these were benevolent actions designed to protect the children. History, however, has shown instead that more than 100,000 children, now called the Stolen Generation, were removed from their families and given to churches and white families. This government action has harbored anger and resentment from the people who had their family members stolen by the government.

One Aborigine living near Alice Springs tells how some 30 children were taken from their parents and divided into three lines. Brothers and sisters were separated as one line of children was taken by the Catholic Church, another by the Anglican Church, and the last by the Methodists. The scars of this horrible action remain in the stories told by older Aborigines today, as the government policy extended to about 1960. The height of the activity was in the 1930s.

Prime Minister Rudd conveyed the nation's remorse and a formal apology for the Stolen Generation by saying:

freedom of religion, speech, press, assembly, conscience, and association. The right to a speedy and public trial is also guaranteed, as is the right to counsel and a trial by jury if desired. The Rosebud Sioux Constitution disallows double jeopardy, which means that a person can't be tried twice for the same crime. It also

> We apologize for the laws and policies of successive Parliaments and governments that have inflicted profound grief, suffering and loss on these our fellow Australians.
>
> We apologize especially for the removal of Aboriginal and Torres Strait Islander children from their families, their communities and their country.
>
> For the pain, suffering and hurt of these Stolen Generations, their descendants and for their families left behind, we say sorry.
>
> To the mothers and the fathers, the brothers and the sisters, for the breaking up of families and communities, we say sorry.
>
> And for the indignity and degradation thus inflicted on a proud people and a proud culture, we say sorry.
>
> We the Parliament of Australia respectfully request that this apology be received in the spirit in which it is offered as part of the healing of the nation.

While this speech may appear as an attempt to end the issues of the Stolen Generation, the prime minister presented it as more of a beginning of a new future. His government has pledged to work to address the problems created by the horrible legislation of the past. Among the options available are reparations. These are payments to people who were damaged by the government policy. Other options are designed to improve the economic, educational, and political status of Aborigines and Torres Strait Islanders and to extend the life span of these people.

provides for the basic political rights to life, liberty, and property. The Tribal Council is elected by members of the Rosebud Sioux and has jurisdiction over the area of the Rosebud Reservation in south-central South Dakota.

ABORIGINAL PEOPLE AND ECONOMIC RIGHTS

While aboriginal people have had ample violations of their political rights, many have fought for and gained the political freedoms they deserve. Some of these efforts have been at the international level, but most have been implemented at local and national levels. Through these concerted efforts, aboriginal people around the world have made giant strides forward in gaining and exercising their political rights during the twentieth century.

Land Ownership

The most important economic issue for aboriginal peoples has been the right to the lands that they once owned. Whether these lands were taken by westward-moving settlers in the United States or by British settlers in Australia or New Zealand, land has been a key issue. Many aboriginal people believed that land could not be owned. This presented a challenge when confronted by Europeans who believed in land ownership. Treaties were signed and broken as native lands were claimed by the more powerful encroaching European cultures.

Aboriginal people faced superior technology and vast numbers of immigrant settlers who moved onto their traditional lands. This caused friction and fighting that resulted in the indigenous people being forced back into smaller and smaller land areas. In addition to their loss of territory, the lands onto which they were forced often had marginal value for agriculture or other economic purposes. This made life very difficult for native peoples. As a result, many problems arose, such as substance abuse, alcoholism, suicide, crime, divorce, and a shortened life span. The psychological impact of their deteriorating situation has been devastating to many aboriginal people.

Over time, the dominant cultures started to replace aboriginal culture and traditions. Sometimes the government would use a heavy-handed public policy to deal with aboriginal people. This would take many forms, as tens of thousands of Native Americans were forced onto reservations. Churches often sent missionaries to "civilize" the indigenous people, thereby taking away a vital element of their culture and spirituality.

Reforms in Aboriginal Policies

Most governments and churches have recognized the errors of these past actions and have sought to address these issues in other more effective and humane ways. For example, the U.S. government saw how reservations were not effective in promoting economic development and improving the life of Native Americans. In 1971, Congress passed the Alaska Native Claims Settlement Act (ANCSA). President Richard Nixon signed the bill, which resolved the largest Native land-claims settlement in U.S. history. The legislation transferred back 44 million acres (approximately 17.8 million hectares) of land to twelve Alaska Native regional corporations (a thirteenth was created later) and more than 200 local village corporations. The settlement also provided for $963 million dollars, which was divided among the corporations. At the same time, this new law ended all other Native land claims in Alaska. Thus, Alaska Natives have had a huge opportunity to advance their economic interests and opportunities.

Although Alaska Natives have been able to settle their land claims, many other indigenous people in the United States and other places have not. New Zealand's prime minister recently pledged to settle all Maori land claims by 2020. However, many Maori remain skeptical. Australia passed the Native Title Act in 1993, which allowed Aborigines and Torres Strait Islander people to file land claims. This act was amended in 2007 in an attempt to speed up the processing of the claims of Aboriginal people to lands. The UNDRIP is clear on the issue of land by stating: "States shall provide effective mechanisms for prevention of and redress of . . . any action which has the aim or effect of dispossessing

MAKING C⊕NNECTI⊕NS

WHAT IS THE STATUS OF ABORIGINAL PEOPLE IN YOUR SOCIETY?

The United States, Canada, Australia, New Zealand, and many other countries have indigenous populations. Many of the issues facing these countries in the past still linger today. Most of these issues are being addressed in some way, but some may be neglected. What aboriginal people live in or near your community? Your region? Your country? After identifying these groups, review the following questions and research the answers to determine their human rights status at present.

- ➡ Do the indigenous groups have any existing land claims? If yes, what is the status of their claims?
- ➡ Have these people preserved their language, spirituality, and other cultural traditions? If so, how?
- ➡ Have these people historically been discouraged or prevented from practicing their language and other important cultural traditions?
- ➡ What is the political status of these indigenous people? What unique problems, if any, do they face in voting or in the courts?
- ➡ Are economic human rights protected? What problems and issues, if any, exist that may not be in accordance with the United Nations Declaration on the Rights of Indigenous Peoples? How are these issues being addressed?
- ➡ What can you do to support the human rights of the indigenous people you have identified?

them of their lands, territories or resources." It is also clear on what should be done if land has been taken. The land should be returned, or, if that is not possible, the indigenous people should be fairly compensated for their loss.

Other Economic Issues

Other economic issues also face aboriginal people. Some seek educational opportunities away from their traditional homelands. They move to urban areas where they gradually become acculturated—they take on many of the characteristics of the dominant culture. Others gain their education and return to their home region to give back to their community. Some societies provide indigenous people with special educational or economic opportunities because of their unique status.

UNDRIP Economic Protections

The range of human rights recognized by the dominant society varies greatly from country to country. Some aboriginal people remain neglected in terms of basic economic human rights. Other countries provide aboriginal people with many opportunities for equality within the larger society. The UN Declaration on the Rights of Indigenous Peoples (UNDRIP) also states other economic rights and protections for indigenous people. Among these are:

- All labor rights established by national and international law
- To protect indigenous children from economic exploitation or work that is hazardous, harmful to their health, or interferes with their education
- Protection from discrimination in labor conditions, salary, or employment
- The right to improvement of their economic, educational, and social conditions
- The right to be actively involved in developing and determining health, housing, and other economic programs affecting them

Native people have also used self-determination and an understanding of their human rights to create new economic opportunities. In the United States, for example, the Indian Gaming Regulatory Act (IGRA) was enacted by Congress in 1988. Since that time, Indian casinos have sprouted up in 28 states. By 2007, there were 423 Indian gaming operations operated by 225 tribes with a net profit of about $26 billion. The casinos have reduced unemployment and poverty on the reservations. And the revenue has supported hundreds of worthwhile tribal programs and developments.

Many economic projects emphasize traditional Native American culture. Tourism, for example, is being developed by many indigenous people. Many tourists seek out cultural information, arts and crafts, and historical sites. Cultural performances take place in communities ranging from Alaska Natives to the Maoris of New Zealand, and tourists flock to these events. In turn, these provide jobs that also preserve the local cultural traditions in music, dance, literature, spirituality, housing, and other areas.

CURRENT EFFORTS TO IMPROVE THE STATUS OF ABORIGINAL PEOPLE

Passage of the UN Declaration on the Rights of Indigenous Peoples in 2007 was a giant step forward in recognizing the special issues of aboriginal people and human rights. However, the UNDRIP is just a piece of paper that can be tossed aside without the vigilance of citizens working to have the rights enforced. Even the four countries (United States, Australia, Canada, and New Zealand) that voted against the UNDRIP are working to make progress in respecting and protecting the human rights of aboriginal people.

Political Action in Canada

In Canada, indigenous peoples are referred to as First Nations in recognition of their special status. Progress has not taken place as fast as desired by First Nations peoples. In 2007, for example, indigenous people led a nationwide protest aimed at ending hunger. The June 29 protest was called Aboriginal Day of Action and served to put pressure on the Canadian government for action on rights related to health, income, and education. This is one of many attempts by Canada's First Nations people to have their human rights issues addressed.

The American Indian Movement

Native Americans have also been very active in the United States in an attempt to have important human rights issues addressed.

Indigenous people of North America have had a long history of struggle. In the United States, American Indians have fought for the U.S. government to recognize their rights. In Canada, the First Nations peoples have demanded action from the Canadian government to improve their health, income, and education rights. Above, aboriginal people protest land claim negotiations in Toronto in 2007.

One such attempt was the American Indian Movement (AIM) of the 1970s. Although this group was controversial and sometimes violent in its political protests, it sought to have many basic human rights issues addressed by the U.S. government. Human rights issues were addressed in their *Trail of Broken Treaties: 20 Point Position Paper* (1972). These included land issues, natural resources, legal jurisdiction over their lands, religious freedom, cultural rights, education, housing, health, and other economic rights. Although many in the media became enamored with AIM's political activities, their 20 points reflect many of the ideas now stated in the UNDRIP.

Discussion still exists outside and inside of Native communities as to whether AIM had a positive or negative impact. In either case, the issues put forth do address important human rights issues, many of which still have not been addressed by the U.S. or state governments.

While many aboriginal rights issues linger, it remains clear that both indigenous people and majority populations have a stake in improving human rights for all. As we have seen, the international community and many nations are working to address the economic, political, social, and other cultural human rights issues that still exist.

GLOBAL CONNECTIONS

The first people in any area have left their legacy and heritage on the lands and their history. Their status as "the first" has usually not been respected by invading settlers who moved onto their lands. The outsiders have seized the traditional lands of aboriginal people and forced them to assimilate or to move onto smaller areas. Accompanying the loss of lands was the loss of culture and spirituality.

An alien culture was forced upon many indigenous people who also lost their political and economic rights. Reform started in the twentieth century and has continued into the twenty-first.

However, progress has been very slow, as the land issues are difficult to figure out—even if there is a will by the majority culture to figure them out. If the dominant culture recognizes rightful land claims, land and other compensation can be used in attempts to fairly address these and other historic economic wrongdoings. Political equality and equality of opportunity have improved during the past century. However, there are still further improvements that are needed to have nations comply with the UNDRIP.

Aboriginal people are not the only ones who have suffered from long-standing human rights violations. Women, too, have often held less power and have not been afforded their equality in human rights. Chapter 6 explores how the path of human rights for women has been traveled.

HUMAN RIGHTS
OF WOMEN

Women have been on the losing end of human rights for much of human history. Men have also doubtlessly suffered throughout history, but with a major difference. This difference is that, traditionally, men have been the primary holders of power and authority in most societies. Whether it was in the churches or mosques, in business or in the halls of government, men traditionally have ruled and women have been relegated to a secondary status. This diminished status has been marked with sexual, physical, and mental abuse; subjugation to men; and unequal pay and working conditions. It has also allowed for a lower political status and even human trafficking. Sadly, many of these atrocities continue today.

This chapter examines the past and some of the progress that women around the world have made in human rights. It also details some of the problems that continue today. It is important to remember that the institutions that have violated the rights of women include some of the most prominent in societies. These include religion, government, business, and even the family. Change remains difficult for societies but is slowly taking place to the benefit of women. Even the United States has been slow in recognizing women's rights. After all, the first viable woman candidate for president, Hillary Clinton, only appeared in the 2008 election. While other societies such as Israel, Pakistan, India, New Zealand, Canada, the United Kingdom, and Germany have had women leaders, the United States has not. Thus, change is difficult not only in traditional societies but in modern ones as well.

SOCIAL AND CULTURAL HUMAN RIGHTS OF WOMEN

Traditional cultural norms (normal activity of a society) and values have placed women at a lower level than men throughout history and across societies. Some exceptions exist, but they are in a distinct minority. Some norms get written into law, but many are unwritten cultural values that a society holds. These norms have frequently allowed men to physically, verbally, or sexually abuse and even assault women. The physical abuse of women, in complete violation of human rights, has been a large social problem in much of the world, including the United States and Canada. Women are the major victims of domestic violence, and societal norms have often supported this despicable behavior.

Domestic Violence

In places like Uzbekistan, government officials often force women to stay in abusive marriages and tell them to just be better wives. Women's shelters in the United States are filled with women seeking protection from violent men for themselves and their children. The cultural norms that encourage and allow these behaviors present a huge human rights challenge for many societies.

Both men and women have challenged these violent behaviors, as laws in the United States and other countries now severely punish those who are guilty of domestic violence. Awareness of the problem has caused more women to report these criminal behaviors, but the problem remains a major issue. The United States has made great efforts and progress in prosecuting those who are abusive.

Women and War

Women are also victimized when wars break out, forcing them from their homes or even their homelands as refugees. The norms of warfare typically violate a wide range of human rights, including the basic right to life. With men doing most of the fighting, the tragedies encountered by women may be even more personal, psychological, and devastating. Rape, sexual assault, and misuse of children are frequently used as military tools. Too frequently there are few if any consequences for the men who criminally violate these women. Even though rape and sexual assault during war are considered war crimes and crimes against humanity, almost none are ever prosecuted. This issue is receiving increased international attention. It also provides an area where citizens can work to influence their governments to enforce laws that protect women from rape and sexual violence.

Women and Cultural Practices

In addition to the cultural elements listed earlier, there are many other cultural practices and beliefs that disallow the human rights of women—including those involved with religions. Many societies believe that women belong at home. In some respects, this sounds fine. But it is only good if a woman is free to choose this option from among others. Some cultures severely restrict women's options by limiting their access to education. Knowledge is power, and uneducated or poorly educated women are largely powerless. This is particularly critical because it places women at a great disadvantage in developing their own economic security.

Some cultural practices are physically harmful to women. They may even encourage or require women to mutilate their own bodies. For example, in Southeast Asia, women from the Kayan tribe have long used brass rings to make their necks appear longer. The rings are added as a girl ages into a woman until

WOMEN, RELIGION, AND HUMAN RIGHTS

Many women are assigned secondary roles in society by their religious faith. This is true of most of the world's major religions, including Islam, Hinduism, and even Christianity. For example, many conservative Christians will not allow women to become ministers, elders, or priests, and many Muslims will not tolerate women in leadership positions. Religious documents and theological arguments were used, and in some cases are still used, to control and subjugate women. Some arguments even shower women with shame simply for being women. For example, some Orthodox Christians still hold women responsible for all sin—even today. At the Council of Macon (France), held in A.D. 500 during the Dark Ages, a vote was taken to determine whether women even possess souls. In the sixth century, Christian philosopher Boethius stated, "Woman is a temple built upon a sewer." Norms developed during that era degraded women in ways that have been difficult to unwind over the centuries. In the sixteenth century, Lutherans debated whether or not women were human! Some of these legacies still impact the role of women today within their faith.

Christian persecution of witches during a three-century period extending from 1500 to 1800 was yet another attempt to control women by shame and degradation. Women accused of witchcraft were persecuted in France, England, and the American colonies, among other places. Some were burned at the stake, and others were hanged or crushed. Tens of thousands of women were killed for being labeled as witches during this era.

Obviously, most churches have evolved tremendously in their attitudes toward women, although to varying degrees. Some faiths, such as Quakers, United Methodists, Presbyterians, and Episcopalians, treat women as full equals to men in church roles and rights. Some others, however, still restrict certain rights and leadership roles for women.

her collarbone is crushed, making the neck appear grotesquely elongated. These women are sometimes called "long-neck" or "giraffe" women, and, sadly, they are now being exploited as a cultural tourist show.

In some African societies, women have their lips stretched or their genitals mutilated. In the past, some Chinese women had their feet bound to keep them small. Corsets were once used in the United States and other countries to keep waists wasp thin. Even today in Western societies, norms dictate what many women do to meet cultural expectations. Tattoos, piercings, slim figures, and even high heels are considered by some as culturally imposed behaviors that pose risks to women. Thus, it is extremely important to investigate and question one's own society to determine the cultural elements that contribute to gender discrimination and harm.

Progress has been slow in many societies. It may be easy to create new laws, but they can be difficult to enforce if the old societal values and norms still exist. When this happens, women continue to lose in the battle for their human rights.

WOMEN AND POLITICAL RIGHTS

Historically, women have generally held little if any formal political power. Even in democracies, women were slow in gaining the fundamental political right to vote. For example, in the United States, women have been able to vote for less than a century. Whereas some states allowed women to vote, the right finally came nationally in 1920 with the passage of the Nineteenth Amendment to the U.S. Constitution. Suffragette Susan B. Anthony was even arrested for trying to vote in an election in 1872 as women fought for this basic political right. On the other hand, the United States allowed women to run for office as early as 1788.

Canadian women gained the right to vote about the same time as their sisters in the United States. Women in Alberta, Manitoba, and Saskatchewan could vote in 1916, and by 1918, the policy extended across the country (except for Quebec). Women

A 12-year-old Thai girl from the Padaung tribe displays her brass neck rings. In the Padaung culture, coils of brass rings are placed on the necks of girls as young as four. Rings are added until the age of 15, at which time the neck coils total 25 and weigh 11 pounds (5 kg).

in Quebec were not allowed to vote until 1940. Some countries were even slower in granting voting rights to women. Mexico finally allowed women to vote in national elections and stand for office in 1953. Even later are Malaysia in 1957, Iran in 1980, Liechtenstein (in Western Europe) in 1984, and Kuwait in 2005. Shockingly, there are still places where women do not have the right to vote. Among these are Vatican City, Saudi Arabia, the United Arab Emirates (UAE), and a few other places. Fortunately, this list is short, and the UAE is planning to make suffrage universal in the near future.

Justice for Women

The justice system is another area where women often have their human rights violated. For example, in Saudi Arabia, unless there are special circumstances, women can't testify at trials. Even in the cases where they do testify, their words are not considered facts. Because of the inferior political status of women, their testimonies in rape cases or when they are assaulted hold little or no weight.

Cases that to Westerners sound absurd often occur in Saudi courts because of the strict application of sharia law (Islamic religious law). For example, a recent case concerned a woman who was in a car alone with a man who was not a relative. The woman was gang raped. Because she violated the separation of the sexes, required by sharia law, she was sentenced to 200 lashes and six months in jail. The country does not even have a law that criminalizes violence against women! In addition, women do not have economic independence and cannot drive or even ride bikes on public roads. This means that they do not have the ability to even escape from an environment where they face physical, sexual, or mental abuse.

Women in Saudi Arabia face legal peril by simply walking down the street. If alone, they might be arrested for prostitution or other moral offenses. They are also subject to arrest if they are found walking with a man who is not their relative. Many cultural practices are written into Saudi law that discriminate

A Saudi woman walks unaccompanied in the street. In Saudi Arabia, women cannot drive. In addition, they are at risk walking alone or with men who are not related to them. The UN has implored Saudi Arabia to improve the human rights of women in the country.

against women or prevent equal opportunity to education, travel, medical care, and job opportunities.

Believe it or not, women can fly airplanes in Saudi Arabia. Hanadi Hindi was the first Saudi woman to become a commercial pilot. She had to seek her education in Jordan, as her country prohibited women from studying to become pilots. She was hired by Prince Alwaleed ibn Talal's Kingdom Holding Company in 2004 to fly corporate jets. The prince had also financed her training in Jordan to help advance the cause of women in Saudi Arabia—but she still cannot legally drive herself to the airport!

To improve human rights for Saudi women, the United Nations, many nongovernmental organizations (NGOs), and various international women's groups are applying pressure upon the Saudi rulers. However, with a very conservative Islamic culture, change is painfully slow.

Many other countries fall far short in providing women basic guarantees of human rights. For example, Mali and Yemen still have laws that require a wife's obedience to her husband. In Afghanistan, many human rights of women have been and continue to be ignored by the Taliban. Under Taliban control, all women were forced to wear the smothering garb of the burqa in public, often against their will. The defense of this law was that men could be corrupted by seeing women's faces. Women endured other human indignities, as well. For example, they were not allowed to be educated over the age of eight and were not allowed to hold jobs outside the home. Their freedom of movement was limited as they couldn't even travel on the same bus as men.

Gender segregation marked daily life, with Taliban women bearing the brunt of the responsibility by sacrificing nearly all freedoms in public. In addition, women who sought advanced schooling and greater involvement in Taliban society were often victimized. Some were even killed for having defied the rigid Taliban rules. Taliban men seek to enforce even the strictest sharia laws and to subjugate all women in Afghan society. The situation has improved somewhat in Afghanistan since the Taliban were ousted from power in 2001. However, renewed efforts by the Taliban to subjugate Afghan and Pakistani women have continued late into the first decade of the twenty-first century.

WOMEN AND ECONOMIC RIGHTS

Women's economic rights also reflect a secondary status across much of the world. Economic rights may include such things as education, freedom of movement, equal opportunity for jobs, the right to own and inherit property, good working conditions, and adequate earnings. Violations of economic human rights can include sexual harassment, slavery, and not being allowed to work outside the home. They also include unequal pay, unreasonable working hours or conditions, poverty, not being able to inherit family property, and other issues. The issues vary widely from country to country and between cultures.

Property Ownership

In the Himalayan nation of Nepal, women long had the right to own property only if they were 35 or older and not married. This has changed slightly, but women must still return family property if they get married. In Chile, laws provide that men in a marriage will manage joint property and the woman's property. Inheritance laws in the 1980s in African nations like Nigeria, Ghana, Kenya, and Zimbabwe did not allow women to own or receive property. This situation has improved with new laws, but many courts in these countries are still not protecting a woman's right to inherit property.

Employment

Many societies have discriminated or still systematically discriminate against women in employment because of reproductive issues. Others hold cultural values against women working outside of the home. A pregnant woman can often encounter difficulties in locating a job and may not advance in her job status because of childbearing. Thus, it is difficult for women to climb the corporate ladder and receive equal pay for equal work.

This often results in what has been called the "glass ceiling." This means that women can see these higher and better-paying jobs, but institutional sexism has denied them the opportunity to hold these top jobs.

U.S. presidential candidate Hillary Clinton talked about the glass ceiling during her concession speech in 2008. During the primary season, she received more than 18 million votes, more than any woman in U.S. history. She reflected back on her historic campaign for the presidency as a woman by saying, "Although

MAKING CONNECTIONS

ARE WOMEN IN YOUR SOCIETY EQUAL TO MEN?

It is easy to look at the role of women in other societies, but it is more difficult to have an honest examination of your own community and society. Cultural, political, and economic rights have greater meaning if they actually apply to your own local community and life. Take time to investigate the following questions by talking with people in your community. Some may take offense to your questions, but understand that they may be caught in a system of cultural values that still places women at a secondary level. Some of these questions are easy to investigate on the Internet, but discussions may reveal more interesting views.

→ What is the percentage of women in elected political positions in your state and local governments?

→ Are there local corporations or government bodies that have women as the chief executive officer?

→ What institutions (such as government or businesses) in your community provide equal pay for women and men?

we weren't able to shatter that highest, hardest glass ceiling this time, thanks to you [the voters] it's got about 18 million cracks in it." Whereas the glass ceiling is still an issue in the United States and other developed societies, women in much of the world cannot even see the top opportunities.

CURRENT REFORMS TO IMPROVE THE STATUS OF WOMEN

Thankfully, there are numerous efforts today to improve the human rights of women. Some attempts are international, but

- → Is it common for men to be homemakers in your community?
- → Do women in your community mainly occupy jobs that are traditionally held by women, or are they active in nontraditional positions as well?
- → Do local churches, including your own, provide women with equal roles and rights?
- → How prevalent are domestic violence and other crimes against women in your community?
- → What resources and institutions are available to protect women in your community?
- → Are there any laws that treat women unequally?
- → Are there cultural norms or values that drive the clothing and physical appearance of women and girls in your community?
- → Is International Women's Day (March 8) celebrated in your community? Why or why not?

Add to these questions as you investigate.

important efforts are also taking place every day in local communities. Various NGOs and governmental organizations often help women achieve and maintain their rights. Among other things, these may include women's shelters, legal resources, and economic efforts designed to assist women. On the local level, there are economic efforts such as the $20,000 microgrant offered to women by Zion Bank in Utah and Idaho. Internationally, the World Bank has used microgrants to allow women to create their own businesses, with some amounts being only a few hundred dollars. These loans have proven to be very successful in helping women to gain economic security for themselves and their families.

On a larger scale, international gatherings are regularly held to address the human rights of women. For example, the Fourth World Conference on Women was held in Beijing, China, in 1995. Here, women developed a platform that called for achieving greater equality and economic opportunity. A Woman's World Conference is slated for Sofia, Bulgaria, in 2010. In addition, a number of international organizations are working to address women's rights. These include efforts by the United Nations, World Bank, and Amnesty International, among others. In addition, March 8 has been designated as International Women's Day and serves to celebrate the political, economic, and social achievements of women.

GLOBAL CONNECTIONS

This chapter is too short to document sufficiently the human rights violations that have been inflicted upon women throughout history and those that still occur today. Many cultural institutions, including those political, economic, and social in nature, still systematically discriminate against women. This is true of the world, and it remains true of the United States, Canada, and Western Europe. Both women and men lose when these discriminatory practices are allowed to continue. True equality involves understanding, respect, and compassion. Both men *and* women deserve to benefit from the human rights guaranteed by the UDHR and by law. It is the responsibility of all citizens to protect these rights because, as China's former leader Mao Tse-tung once said, "Women hold up half the sky." Cultures, governments, churches, businesses, and families all benefit when opportunities are open to all regardless of their gender, sexual orientation, race, ethnic, social, or political status. Much more remains to be accomplished.

HUMAN RIGHTS OF OTHER MINORITIES

Aboriginal groups and women are not the only people who have had difficult histories in terms of human rights. The oppressed also include other minorities. These groups may be ethnic, economic, political, religious, or social in nature. In some African countries, certain tribes may be a minority in the country's culture. In India, the traditional castes present an out-dated class structure that persists in discriminating against those known as the "untouchables," or Dalits. We'll explore the Dalits' situation later in this chapter.

Political minorities can also suffer, such as those people who opposed Zimbabwe's Robert Mugabe in the 2008 elections. Many of these political opponents were arrested, physically harassed, intimidated, and even murdered—just because they supported Mugabe's opponent, Morgan Tsvangirai. Others may be economic or social outcasts, such as the Roma (Gypsy) people in Europe or the homeless people in the United States and elsewhere.

Many of these minorities have little or no political or economic clout and have often suffered under the rule of the majority in their countries. In democracies such as the United States and Canada, the majority rules but minority rights are still protected. The quest has been to have rights and freedoms equally applied to all people in a society regardless of their gender, or economic, social, political, ethnic, or other status. In this respect, many democracies and even nondemocracies fall far short of actually providing equal protection for the rights of all.

POLITICAL HUMAN RIGHTS

Young democracies and dictatorships often view political opposition in a narrow manner. Without traditions that respect democratic institutions and practices, many of these societies actually persecute members of the political opposition. In Zimbabwe, the political opposition in 2008 likely represented a majority of the population. However, the heavy-handed tactics of Robert Mugabe repeatedly trampled over the human rights of opponents. The rights to life and freedom of assembly, association, expression, and the press were repeatedly violated, regardless of what the Universal Declaration of Human Rights (UDHR) states.

POLITICAL OPPRESSION OF MINORITIES

Zimbabwe is not the only place where political oppression of minorities has taken place. Russia, China, Sudan, Burma (Myanmar), Uzbekistan, North Korea, Angola, Saudi Arabia, and many other places are operating well below UN standards in terms of protecting political rights. Even the United States was criticized by the international community for failing to provide impartial, timely, and fair trials for the September 11, 2001, terrorist suspects held at the Guantanamo Bay detention camp in Cuba. This situation was later deemed unconstitutional by a 5–4 vote of the

U.S. Supreme Court in June 2008. The decision confirmed that the detainees were entitled to the protection of the U.S. Constitution. This U.S. court ruling for justice stands in stark contrast to the al Qaeda terrorists who massacred more than 3,000 innocent civilians on September 11.

Many also suffer by living in political systems where the rule of man prevails over law. Thus, nations as diverse as Colombia, Angola, North Korea, Saudi Arabia, Iraq, Bangladesh, Togo, and far too many others are tainted by not having the rule of law prevail equally for all citizens. Their arbitrary rule allows for political shenanigans that destroy the political freedoms of people within the society. True democratic rule, marked by justice,

MAKING C⊕NNECTI⊕NS

IN YOUR JUDGMENT...

In this book, you have examined human rights and issues related to indigenous people, women, and other minorities. Use your expertise and research skills to examine the following questions about political, social, economic, or ethnic minorities.

- What political, social, economic, or ethnic minorities exist in your country or locality?
- What human rights challenges do these people still face, if any?
- What current activities are being conducted to address these challenges?
- What government policies have been most successful in improving the human rights of these minorities?
- What do you believe is the most pressing human rights issue facing a minority in your community? How do you believe this issue could best be addressed?

is the answer for resolving these human rights issues. However, the international community has often been slow or ineffective in addressing problems when they arise.

ECONOMIC HUMAN RIGHTS

The right to earn a living and take care of your family is not only foundational but essential. Having an equal opportunity to get and keep a job is also fundamental. Thus, discrimination against an individual because of his or her ethnicity, religion, or where he or she lives is plainly wrong and against the UDHR. Not being able to get a job and be paid equally for the same work only increases poverty among those minorities who are discriminated against in a society.

The poor, those who are economically disadvantaged, are also often disadvantaged in other ways. Money means power in most societies. The poor fall prey to "the system," as they do not have the money and sometimes the education necessary to protect their rights. The poor are found around the world and are sometimes women, indigenous peoples, an ethnic minority, the handicapped, or the elderly. Children also suffer, as they are not financially independent and are reliant upon others for their economic well-being.

The Roma People

The Roma people face many economic and social issues. These people were originally from India but arrived in Europe about five centuries ago. Traditionally called "Gypsies," the Roma are found around the world today, but most often in Europe. Historically, they were nomadic, a factor that often imposes difficulties on a society. Nomads move from place to place, sometimes seasonally, to maintain their lifestyle. The Roma have developed a strong group identity because of this lifestyle.

The life of a nomad isn't easy in the twenty-first century. As a nomad, a number of challenges occur: How are your children

A Gypsy woman begs with her young child. An ethnic group that has been consistently persecuted throughout much of history, the nomadic Roma are fighting to maintain their culture. In 2005, several European countries joined together to form the Decade of Roma Inclusion initiative, whose goal is to improve the welfare and living conditions of the Roma people by 2015.

educated? How can you get and keep a job? How do you get health care? The Roma face many of these challenges and often live in poverty. Persecution of the Roma has been frequent in Europe, primarily because they do not want to assimilate. Discrimination against the Roma persists in Europe today. But it was at its worst during World War II, when half a million Roma disappeared in Nazi concentration camps. Recent efforts have tried to force the Roma to integrate into the larger societies. However, these efforts denied the Roma the right to preserve their language and other elements of their culture. Thus, hostility against the Roma remains a major problem today throughout much of Europe.

Traditionally, persecution of the Roma has been because of their poverty and their culture. Discrimination against the poor exists in many countries. The plight of the homeless is fraught with danger and neglect. Many will argue that the homeless bear some responsibility for their situation. But others believe that a just society must still protect their rights regardless of whether or not they are responsible for their condition. This belief is advanced in the UDHR by rights that include "the right to life, liberty, and security."

SOCIAL AND CULTURAL HUMAN RIGHTS

Religion and other elements of culture have placed some at a distinct disadvantage in terms of their human rights. Religious examples are evident in Ireland, the Middle East, the Balkans, and many other areas. Sunnis battle against Shiites in Iraq, and Catholics and Protestants have a long-simmering feud in Northern Ireland. The 1990s saw the former country of Yugoslavia explode in a conflict between Croats, Serbs, and Bosniaks. This conflict also had religious linkages, as thousands of Orthodox Christians (Serbs), Roman Catholics (Croats), and Muslims (Bosniaks) died or were victimized during the war. In Africa, the ethnic tribes of nations such as Nigeria have long served to divide the country between the Ibo, Yoruba, and Hausa factions. Many people in Nigeria (and elsewhere in Africa) hold their ethnic identity to be more important than their national citizenship.

India's Caste System

India's caste system has been outlawed by the country's constitution since 1947, but many of the old practices still linger within the culture. The caste system identified social classes mainly by heredity. People were born into a caste and died as members of the same caste. Their hope was to be reborn in a higher class, as caste mobility was limited. However, outside of the caste system were people (outcasts) who were long referred to as the "untouchables." These people are now referred to as Dalits and number nearly 165 million in India. Traditionally, the

REPRESSION IN TIBET

Beijing, China, hosted the 2008 Summer Olympics. Before the games began, the Olympic torch was carried around the world and even to the top of Mount Everest on its 130-day journey to Beijing. In contrast to the Olympic spirit, many demonstrators appeared along the route of the Olympic torch to protest. What caused these demonstrations?

The answer requires a bit of history, politics, and geography. Tibet is located on the Tibetan Plateau between the huge and powerful countries of India and China. Its high elevation, banked by the towering Himalayas to the southwest, has served to make it a remote location because of the historical difficulty in traveling there.

Although China had traditional claims on Tibet, the Tibetans successfully overthrew the Chinese in 1912. Tibet claimed to be independent during the early twentieth century, but China considered it to be a special territory. China successfully invaded Tibet in 1950, and in 1951 it became a national autonomous (semi-independent) region of Communist China. The Chinese then attempted to control the strong influence of Buddhism and the Dalai Lama, and tried to institute communes (large government farms) as a land reform. The Tibetans resisted, and a war broke out against the Chinese in 1959.

China was ruthless in putting down the Tibetan rebellion. Meanwhile, the Dalai Lama escaped to India and charged that China had committed genocide. China has ruled Tibet since that time as the Tibetan Autonomous Region. Since the rebellion in 1959, Tibetans have continued to complain about human rights violations. These complaints include discrimination, political persecution, religious persecution, arbitrary arrests, torture, and genocide. On March 10, 2008, the forty-ninth anniversary of the failed 1959 Tibetan rebellion, more than 300 Tibetan monks protested against the Chinese government.

Dalits worked with leather, animal carcasses, or human and animal waste, or as street cleaners and other positions considered undesirable. Because of their work, the Dalits were considered

They were protesting the detainment of other monks who had been held by China since 2007.

The fourteenth Dalai Lama has played a prominent role in the world today and is viewed as a positive moral force by millions of people in the international community. His inspiration has fueled Tibetans to keep and practice their Buddhist beliefs in the face of strong repression by the Chinese government. He stated to the world that the protests were caused by Tibetan discontent. Shortly afterward, the monks' protests were squelched, but the protests had been viewed by the world. The reaction fostered demonstrations for Tibetans during the carrying of the Olympic flame in Greece, France, the United Kingdom, Japan, the United States, and other countries. Pro-China factions also showed their support for China and the Olympics as the issue of Tibet increased the intensity of feelings by many Chinese nationals at home and overseas.

While the human rights issues have drawn international attention, China closed free media access to Tibet shortly after the March 2008 protests. This made international monitoring of the human rights status of Tibetans more difficult. China and Tibet continue to differ on their views regarding the importance and existence of human rights. As this Tibetan case study shows, identifying and changing human rights situations is a very complex process fraught with risk to those who seek to make the issue public. Taking human rights issues public frequently puts individuals at further risk of imprisonment, torture, and even death. People willing to carry these issues forward with the associated risks are courageous heroes who often become local or international martyrs. Tibet has had many courageous heroes and martyrs.

Supporters of the National Confederation of Dalit Organizations demand equal rights in a protest in New Delhi, India, in 2009. Previously known as "untouchables," Dalits still encounter a degree of discrimination in India. Even though the constitution forbids it, long-standing cultural perceptions are difficult to change.

polluted and not to be touched—thus, the term *untouchable*. As untouchables, Dalits traditionally were not even allowed to have their shadow fall upon a person in a caste.

India's cultural attitudes toward the Dalits and their rights have improved, especially in urban areas. However, the problem persists in rural areas where customs change very slowly. Indian leaders like Mohandas Gandhi and Jawaharlal Nehru, India's first prime minister, worked to eliminate the discrimination and stigma of untouchability. However, in 2006, Prime Minister Manmohan Singh publicly recognized the parallels still existing in India between untouchability and apartheid. Thus, the problem of discrimination against the Dalits still continues even though

India's constitution and leadership are supportive of their rights. This problem continues because it is deeply ingrained in some elements of the culture, including India's dominant Hindu faith. Much work remains to be done.

CURRENT EFFORTS TO IMPROVE THE STATUS OF MINORITIES

The international community and many countries today are working to improve the status and well-being of minorities. When justice applies to all equally, minorities of all types win—as does the majority. Whether this means having an equal opportunity for education and a job, equal pay for equal work, equal political rights, or equal treatment in other ways, justice provides for equal opportunity. What any person does with equal opportunity is the responsibility of the individual. His or her success or failure should be based solely on merit. Progress has been slow, but most societies recognize the importance of having all their citizens provided with equal access to success. Nations win when their people win.

WHAT HUMAN RIGHTS ISSUES FACE PEOPLE TODAY?

The second half of the twentieth century saw renewed efforts to address human rights problems and challenges. The United Nations established international standards for human rights, and most of the world community signed onto these agreements. However, as seen earlier, flagrant abuses of human rights still took place in the late twentieth century in places like Rwanda, Cambodia, and the former Yugoslavia. In each of these cases, the international community was painfully slow in inter-vening—often far too late for local populations who fell victim to the abuses and atrocities.

The twenty-first century brought a new millennium and hope for a better future for humankind. What has happened in the first decade of this new millennium with respect to protecting human rights? What human rights issues currently confront humanity? These and other questions are considered in this chapter as we focus upon contemporary issues in human rights.

CONTEMPORARY HUMAN RIGHTS ISSUES

Sadly, the abuses of human rights did not end with the twentieth century. Tragically, old patterns reemerged in various parts of the world, and many others carried over to the dawn of the new century. They include executions outside of the judicial process, torture, unfair trials, and prisoners detained without being charged. Terrorism, ethnic or religious cleansing, and people "disappearing" are included in the list of continuing political rights issues that have been identified by Amnesty International. These continue to take place even though there is strong agreement in the international community about the need to protect civil and political rights.

Modern Slavery

Even slavery has not ended with the twentieth century. Tragically, it appears in many forms, such as slave trade, sale of human organs, sale of children, child labor, prostitution, and pornography. Most of these victims come from the poorest social classes and include those who have little access to institutions and protections that may be available. Children are also forced to fight as warriors in some places, while many women and children are pushed into prostitution in places like Thailand, Uganda, India, the Philippines, and the United Arab Emirates. Prostitution is legal in Canada, Mexico, and most countries in Western Europe. It is regulated under strictly limited conditions, however, so that people will not be forced into the sex trade.

Social Human Rights

Social human rights enumerated in the Universal Declaration of Human Rights are still not fully agreed upon in the international community. Some believe that these rights are too much of a burden for a society to implement. They include education, food, health care, employment, and other things listed in the International Covenant on Economic, Social and Cultural Rights (ICESCR). Thus, the application and enforcement of these social rights in the new century has also been sporadic. Because of this, in many societies children, especially girls, are inadequately educated, and many people suffer from malnutrition and unemployment.

With all of the existing issues and others, the quest to remove human rights abuses has necessarily continued into the

MAKING CONNECTIONS

WHICH HUMAN RIGHTS ISSUES ARE MOST SERIOUS TODAY?

This chapter has identified many human rights issues that are of concern today. Use your knowledge and research to investigate the following issues and determine what human rights issue is of most importance to you.

- Use the Universal Declaration of Human Rights as a guide and identify current human rights issues in the world.
- Pick three to five human rights issues that you believe are important to you.
- Research these issues to determine where the issues are a problem, the history and differing viewpoints on the issues, who is interested in the issues, and how these issues are currently being addressed.
- Select the human rights issue that is of greatest importance to you.
- Design an action plan of political and other activities that you can do to help address the issue you selected.

twenty-first century. The locations may change, but the problems remain the same as injustice, unequal opportunity, poverty, and discrimination continue to plague humankind.

MODERN HUMAN RIGHTS PROBLEMS

Women, aboriginal people, and other minorities continue to be most affected by human rights abuses. Although there are many modern human rights issues that merit discussion, only a few can be discussed on these pages.

Hunger and Poverty

Hunger and poverty are two basic issues that fundamentally affect people around the world today. With the world's population nearing 7 billion people and energy costs rising, food has become more difficult for the poor to obtain. Bread for the World estimates that nearly 900 million people across the world are hungry and that 16,000 children die each day from hunger. The organization states that "hunger is the most extreme form of poverty." It threatens the most basic right of a person—the right to life. Adequate food and clean water are basic to meeting this essential right. Education and economic well-being are keys to people being able to meet these and other basic needs. Nearly a billion people around the world live in poverty, and poverty causes hunger.

Water is also an essential need for life. Clean Water for the World reported in 2008 that 1.8 million children die each year from diarrhea caused by dirty drinking water. They further reported that one child dies every 15 seconds from water-related diseases. The World Health Organization estimates that 1.1 billion people do not have access to clean drinking water.

War and Terrorism

War and Terrorism also continue to violate the basic right to life. In 2008, wars and fighting were taking place in many locations. The United States remained active in Afghanistan and Iraq as a result of the attack on September 11, 2001. Fighting bordering on civil war has occurred in such places as Lebanon, Iraq, Sri Lanka, and Sudan. Military fighting also took place between Eritrea and Djibouti, Israel and the Gaza Strip, Ethiopia and Somalia, and in many other locations. History has shown that, when wars and armed conflicts happen, human rights are routinely violated. These include atrocities such as torture, rape, murder, and genocide. Terrorists have also continued their heinous attacks in Iraq, Afghanistan, Israel, Pakistan, Nigeria, the Philippines, Thailand, India, and other locations around the world. On top of the actual attacks, al Qaeda continues to threaten Western Europe, Canada, and the United States with further attacks.

Other Human Rights Violations

Other rights continue to be trampled over in the twenty-first century. The freedom of religion continues to be a major source of conflict. Many, including extremist Islamic terrorists, continue in their efforts to force their beliefs upon others. Some conflicts simmer just below the surface in places like Bosnia and Herzegovina, Kosovo, Northern Ireland, and the Middle East. In Iraq, the division between Sunni and Shiite Muslims has resulted in a renewed form of ethnic cleansing in Baghdad and other communities around the country. Outsiders, including Iran, continue to feed the conflict and division in Iraq in order to gain political and religious advantages in the region. It is estimated that between 600,000 and 700,000 people have died since the fighting began in Iraq. Most of the victims have been innocent civilians.

Political Rights Violated

In addition, human rights abuses also continue with political rights being steadfastly repressed in Zimbabwe, Tibet, Myanmar (Burma), Egypt, Kenya, and other locations. World-famous political prisoner and human rights advocate Aung San Suu Kyi was still a political prisoner in Burma in 2009. She has been detained by the military dictatorship since 1989. Journalists were still being

Family members of a 13-year-old car bomb victim cry over his coffin in the Shiite holy city of Najaf, Iraq, in 2009. The human right of religious freedom continues to be violated in parts of the world, particularly in the Middle East, where extremist Islamists use terrorist tactics to force their beliefs on others.

arrested or intimidated in violation of the freedom of expression and right to disseminate ideas through the media. The persecution, repression, or imprisonment of journalists took place in Belarus, Somalia, Sri Lanka, and Egypt. Political dissent was also stifled in Syria, the Balkans, and numerous other locations.

Thus, the files are filled with new and continuing human rights issues that must be addressed. The number of pages devoted to identifying and explaining contemporary human rights issues will always be inadequate in describing the human horror, suffering, and devastation that these violations inflict upon people. While much remains to be accomplished, there are also important efforts designed to address the human rights problems now facing humanity.

EFFORTS TO ADDRESS CONTEMPORARY HUMAN RIGHTS ISSUES

Despite the world's many human rights problems, there are many exciting efforts taking place to identify and address issues when they arise. Thousands of nongovernmental organizations (NGOs) are working at the local, regional, national, and global levels to address human rights deficiencies. Among these are organizations such as Amnesty International, Human Rights Watch, Global Exchange, Advocates International, Forum 18, International League for Human Rights, and Freedom Watch. NGO activities range from helping the world community recognize human rights violations to conducting activities on-site designed to address immediate needs. Other international organizations such as the International Red Cross and Red Crescent, CARE, Project HOPE, and Action Against Hunger provide assistance in times of peril, such as war, famine, or natural disasters.

Government and international organizations also are vitally important in promoting and preserving human rights. Most democratic societies have public policies designed to protect the rights of individuals. The international community has been slow to advance the agenda declared by the Universal Declaration of Human Rights (UDHR), but the response is improving. One important effort in this area started in April 2008 with the UN Human Rights Council Universal Periodic Review (UPR). This group is charged with conducting periodic reviews of all countries that are members of the United Nations to determine the extent of their compliance with the UDHR. Forty-eight nations were reviewed in the first year of the program, with the rest to be reviewed during the following three years.

The United Nations Human Rights Council adopted a new legal device in 2008 for individuals who believe that their economic, social, or cultural rights have been violated. People will now be able to have their case decided directly by the UN Committee on Economic, Social and Cultural Rights. This means that human rights victims can seek justice in a legal process outside of their own country's governmental structure. This ability greatly strengthens the tools available to human rights victims who are usually powerless within their own society.

The United Nations and other governmental organizations also assist in meeting basic human rights such as the right to life. For example, the United Nations Children's Fund (UNICEF) works to protect the rights and lives of children. It also provides special assistance to children during war, after disasters, or

GENOCIDE: STILL HAPPENING TODAY?

As a new millennium approached, the world waited and hoped that the horror called genocide would be left on the pages of history books and not repeated in the new era. During the twentieth century, genocide claimed 150 million lives. In Rwanda alone, genocide that occurred in 1994 may have claimed a million lives. The world hoped that there would be no more of this heinous killing.

As the dawn of the twenty-first century appeared, however, genocide again raised its ugly head. This time horror struck Sudan, an impoverished nation in northeast Africa with 40 million people. In 2003, fighting broke out in the Darfur region of the country. Nearly 2 million people were displaced from their homes, and more than 250,000 fell victims of the new millennium's first major genocide. The term *ethnic cleansing* reappeared. George Clooney, an actor and human rights activist, properly warned the United Nation's Security Council in 2006 that, "For you it's called ethnic cleansing. But make no mistake—it is the first genocide of the 21st century. And if it continues unchecked it will not be the last." In 2008, Clooney was appointed by UN secretary general Ban Ki-moon as a United Nations Messenger of Peace. In this position he will officially work to draw attention to genocide and other human rights problems.

trapped in poverty. Through its efforts, it is working to protect children in 191 countries from violence, hunger, inequality, exploitation, and disease. Other agencies of the United Nations, such as the World Health Organization, work to protect people from threats to their lives while other international organizations operate at the regional or global level.

HOLDING WAR CRIMINALS ACCOUNTABLE

On the punitive side, efforts to bring war criminals to justice continue. Increasingly, those found guilty of war crimes are being punished. Truth and reconciliation processes in places such as South Africa and Morocco have shown great merit. In Morocco, great strides have been made in having the truth about human rights violations in the country exposed. The nation watched their televisions spellbound as the tales unfolded of people disappearing and being tortured during King Hassan II's reign in the late twentieth century. Reconciliation included not only compensation for victims but also major human rights reforms in the kingdom led by King Mohammed VI. It was his father, King Hassan II, who had committed the human rights violations. Leaders such as King Mohammed VI have given hope to people around the world who value honesty and straightforwardly address abuses. His leadership is unprecedented in the region and may provide a model for others seeking human rights reform though transparency, truth, and finally reconciliation.

THE FUTURE OF HUMAN RIGHTS

L ooking ahead to see what the twenty-first century holds for human rights is a very inexact science. Some futurists use a process of examining the possible, probable, and preferred futures. The possible futures would include examining the wide range of scenarios that *could* happen. Thus, the range of possible futures for human rights could be very broad. This could present a wide variety of events that make it much better, or much worse, than the twentieth century, during which 150 million died as a result of genocide.

In contrast, the probable future takes a historical view to see where we are today and projects what will *likely* happen if we stay on the present path. It is more evolutionary than revolutionary in its analysis. Using this method, one could project that, starting with the agreements reached by the international community in the second half of the twentieth century, human rights will receive more attention and protection. One could also project that atrocities would decline and perpetrators of these events would be held accountable in international tribunals. However, the probable future could also hold further genocide and inaction by an international community that is often slow to respond.

The preferred future is the one that we would *hope* would be fulfilled. Some may view it as a dream, others as our goal as humans. In this vision, the human rights listed by the United Nations in various documents including the Universal Declaration of Human Rights (UDHR) would become a reality for all people in all countries. Those who violate the human rights of others would be brought to justice and held accountable if found guilty. Skeptics say that this is not human nature, while others say we must continue toward the preferred scenario to survive.

A LOOK AT THE PITFALLS

The efforts to advance human rights face many pitfalls and challenges. Those in power illegitimately often oppose common people gaining political rights as provided in the Universal Declaration of Human Rights. Former secretary general of the United Nations Kofi Annan reaffirms this idea by saying, "It was never the people who complained of the universality of human rights, nor did the people consider human rights as a Western or Northern imposition. It was often their leaders who did so."

This pitfall also exists in democracies, as fear can be used as a tactic to have citizens give up rights that are provided by their own constitutions. Many suggest this happened in the United States after the violent attack by al Qaeda on the World Trade Center and the Pentagon in 2001. As a result of the attack, politicians used the fear associated with the attack to decrease the privacy of Americans. Many accepted this loss of rights, as they were told it would help to identify and arrest terrorists. It also gave new powers to the government that decreased the right to privacy. History has shown repeatedly that people will sacrifice rights when they are afraid. Thus, even in democracies, citizens must be vigilant in protecting political human rights. As

Burmese democracy and human rights advocate Aung San Suu Kyi has said, "Fear is not the natural state of civilized people."

Another pitfall is the reluctance of the international community to intervene in circumstances when there are gross violations of human rights. This tendency allows problems to fester until they become violent, with many people suffering and even losing their lives. The UN and other organizations are often reluctant to get involved in the internal matters of member states because of national sovereignty (independence). However, the words in the UDHR also present a challenge to organizations such as the United Nations. Are human rights just words on paper, or are they ideas that the organizations

Displaced Sudanese women unload their belongings in a refugee camp in 2009. Although it may be tempting for the international community to remain neutral, it is important to remember that those whose human rights are violated often do not have the power to help themselves.

and member nations will take action to protect? This pitfall often contributes to human rights violations as the inaction of the UN and other organizations serves to bolster the confidence of tyrants.

WHAT PEOPLE HAVE SAID ABOUT HUMAN RIGHTS

Countless words have been written about human rights. Many are worthy of sharing on these pages, as they both inspire and help clarify our thinking. Here are a few sound bites on human rights—do you understand their meaning?

- "I am the inferior of any man whose rights I trample underfoot." —Horace Greeley
- "Peace can only last where human rights are respected, where the people are fed, and where individuals and nations are free." —Dalai Lama
- "We hold these truths to be self-evident, that all men are created equal; that they are endowed by their Creator with certain inalienable rights; that among these are Life, Liberty, and the pursuit of happiness." —Thomas Jefferson
- "In giving rights to others which belong to them, we give rights to ourselves." —John F. Kennedy
- "Please use your freedom to promote ours." —Aung San Suu Kyi
- "Whenever I hear anyone arguing for slavery, I feel a strong impulse to see it tried on him personally." —Abraham Lincoln
- "An injustice committed against anyone is a threat to everyone." —Montesquieu
- "No man is above the law and no man below it." —Theodore Roosevelt
- "I am not interested in picking up crumbs of compassion thrown from the table of someone who considers himself my master. I want the full menu of rights." —Desmond Tutu

A third pitfall is the tendency of people to be in denial about human rights problems, whether global in scope or in their own backyard. Discrimination in some form is nearly universal. Perhaps it is directed against women, indigenous people, or

➡ "I swore never to be silent whenever human beings endure suffering and humiliation. We must always take sides. Neutrality helps the oppressor, never the victim. Silence encourages the tormentor, never the tormented." —Elie Wiesel

➡ "Freedom means the supremacy of human rights everywhere. Our support goes to those who struggle to gain those rights or keep them." —Franklin Roosevelt

➡ "We could not have peace, or an atmosphere in which peace could grow, unless we recognized the rights of individual human beings . . . their importance, their dignity . . . and agreed that was the basic thing that had to be accepted throughout the world." —Eleanor Roosevelt

➡ "The only way to make sure people you agree with can speak is to support the rights of people you don't agree with." —Eleanor Holmes Norton

➡ "The only thing necessary for the persistence of evil is for enough good people to do nothing." —Unknown

➡ "Never doubt that a small group of thoughtful committed citizens can change the world—indeed it is the only thing that ever does." —Margaret Meade

➡ "You must not lose faith in humanity. Humanity is an ocean; if a few drops of the ocean are dirty, the ocean does not become dirty." —Mohandas Gandhi

➡ "It's really a wonder that I haven't dropped all my ideals, because they seem so absurd and impossible to carry out. Yet I keep them, because in spite of everything I still believe that people are really good at heart." —Anne Frank

homosexuals. Or it may be against those of other religions or ethnicities, the poor, or the handicapped. It is a daily occurrence that is seemingly tolerated. Countering this denial requires work and action from citizens and leaders in all societies around the world. Political pressure provides proactive processes against the perpetrators of these violations.

A fourth pitfall is that the victims of human rights violations often have little or no political or economic power to improve their situation. The action of neighbors and the international community is necessary to intervene in situations such as Zimbabwe and Sudan, as the impoverished citizens are nearly powerless.

THE ROLE OF THE CITIZEN

The role of the citizen is much like being a homeowner. If your roof starts to leak, you fix the problem before it gets bigger and floods your home. The same holds true in protecting human rights. If a problem shows up—act! Do not wait for the problem to show up on your doorstep before taking appropriate action.

MAKING CONNECTIONS

HOW ARE THE RIGHTS OF CHILDREN BEING PROTECTED?

Children are protected under rights identified by the United Nations. Children are among the powerless in societies, as they do not even possess the right to vote. What rights do you have as a youthful citizen of your nation and the world? Identify your rights by researching your nation's constitution and local laws, and the UN Convention on the Rights of the Child. Identify and list the rights provided through these sources.

By then, it is already too late. As the American philosopher Noam Chomsky has stated, "States are not moral agents, people are, and can impose moral standards on powerful institutions." Stated another way, Brazilian educator Paulo Freire said, "Washing one's hands of the conflict between the powerful and the powerless means to side with the powerful, not to be neutral."

Thus, it is clear that *your* role and that of other citizens throughout the global community is the most important factor in shaping the future of human rights. U.S. Medal of Freedom winner Roger Nash Baldwin sums up our role as citizens by saying, "Silence never won rights. They are not handed down from above; they are forced by pressures from below." If nothing else, the stark number—150 million dead because of genocide in the twentieth century—should motivate us as citizens to act. In 2008, the world marked the sixtieth anniversary of the Universal Declaration of Human Rights. We know the history; what will *you* help the future to be?

GLOSSARY

aboriginal people   The first people to settle and occupy a land area.

apartheid   "Separateness" in the Afrikaans language. Describes a government policy in South Africa advanced by the racially white National Party that instituted legal separation based on race.

culture   The totality of a people's way of life, including their language, religion, social interactions, diet, material traits, arts, and values.

ethnic cleansing   The forced and systematic removal of an ethnic group from their home area by any means.

ethnicity   A group of people bound by cultural ties.

ex post facto law   A situation where an individual does something that is not against the law but, afterward, a law is passed making the act illegal. Thus, there was no law against the act at the time it was committed.

genocide   The planned and systematic destruction and annihilation of a particular group of people.

human rights   The rights and freedoms that all people are entitled to simply because they are human.

International Covenant on Civil and Political Rights (ICCPR)   A UN agreement developed in 1966 and implemented by signatories in 1976. It identifies protected civil and political rights.

International Covenant on Economic, Social and Cultural Rights (ICESCR)   United Nations treaty adopted in 1966 and implemented in 1976 that identifies protected economic, social, and cultural rights.

libel   A false published statement that damages a person's reputation.

nongovernmental organizations (NGOs)   Organizations not within government that work to protect human rights or improve social issues.

norms   The typical or normal cultural activity of a society.

rule of law   A political system in which the laws of a society apply equally to all in the society, even leaders.

rule of man   A political system in which laws are applied unequally, with some in the society above the law and not held accountable under the law.

slander   The act of saying something untrue and damaging to another person's reputation.

social contract   An agreement between the government and the governed that defines and limits the rights of both parties.

sovereignty   The right of a country to self-govern without outside interference.

tribunal   An international court used to hold war crime trials.

truth and reconciliation process   A procedure used to expose human rights violations and remedy victims. The process has been used in South Africa and Morocco.

UN Declaration on the Rights of Indigenous Peoples (UNDRIP)   An agreement adopted by the UN General Assembly in 2007 that outlines the rights and freedoms of indigenous peoples.

UN Human Rights Council Universal Periodic Review (UPR)   A periodic review conducted on all countries who are members of the UN to determine the extent of their compliance with the UDHR.

Universal Declaration of Human Rights (UDHR)   Adopted agreement of the United Nations that lists human rights and freedoms that are protected.

BIBLIOGRAPHY

Buergenthal, Thomas, Dinah Shelton, and David P. Stewart. *International Human Rights in a Nutshell*. St. Paul, MN: West Publishing Company, 2002.

Cahn, Steven M. *On Liberty*. New York and Oxford: Rowman & Littlefield Publishers, Inc., 2005.

Clapham, Andrew. *Human Rights: A Very Short Introduction*. New York: Oxford University Press, 2007.

Donnelly, Jack. *Universal Human Rights in Theory and Practice*. Ithaca, NY: Cornell University Press, 1989.

Forsythe, David P. *Human Rights in International Relations*. Cambridge: Cambridge University Press, 2006.

Hayden, Patrick. *The Philosophy of Human Rights*. St. Paul, MN: Paragon House Publishers, 2001.

Hunt, Lynn. *Inventing Human Rights: A History*. New York: W.W. Norton, 2007.

Ishay, Micheline. *The History of Human Rights: From Ancient Times to the Globalization Era*. Berkeley: University of California Press, 2008.

Lauren, Paul Gordon. *The Evolution of International Human Rights: Visions Seen*. Philadelphia: University of Pennsylvania Press, 2003.

Smith, Rhona K. *Textbook on International Human Rights*. New York: Oxford University Press, 2007.

Steiner, Henry, and Philip Alston. *International Human Rights in Context: Law, Politics, Morals*. New York: Oxford University Press, 2000.

Tutu, Desmond. *No Future Without Forgiveness*. London: Trafalgar Square, 1999.

FURTHER RESOURCES

Amnesty International

http://www.amnesty.org

This site provides an array of resources regarding the status of human rights around the world as the organization works to protect human rights.

Electronic Information System for International Law (EISIL)

http://www.eisil.org/index.php?sid=421415088&t=sub_ pages&cat=185

Presents a wide selection of human rights information including sections on women, aboriginal people, and minorities.

Human Rights Watch

http://www.hrw.org

Home page of Human Rights Watch, which works to protect human rights around the world.

United Nations

http://www.un.org/rights

This site provides basic UN documents on human rights along with treaties and tribunals.

United States Department of State

http://www.state.gov/g/drl/hr

Provides an overview of the U.S. position on human rights.

Witness

http://www.witness.org/index.php

Organizational Web site where people around the world submit videos and pictures of human rights abuses.

PICTURE CREDITS

INDEX

ABOUT THE AUTHOR

DOUGLAS A. PHILLIPS is a lifetime educator, writer, and consultant who has worked and traveled in more than 100 countries on six continents. From Alaska to Argentina and from Madagascar to Mongolia, Phillips has worked in education as a middle school teacher, administrator, curriculum developer, and author, and as a trainer of educators who are working for human rights in countries around the world. He has also worked with Native Americans in the United States. Phillips has served as the president of the National Council for Geographic Education, and he has received the Outstanding Service Award from the National Council for the Social Studies along with numerous other awards. He has traveled widely around the world and understands the importance and complexity of human rights in the world today.

 # ABOUT THE EDITOR

CHARLES F. GRITZNER is Distinguished Professor of Geography at South Dakota State University in Brookings. He began college teaching and conducting geographic research in 1960. In addition to teaching, he enjoys travel, writing, working with teachers, and sharing his love of geography with readers. As a senior consulting editor and frequent author for Chelsea House Publishers' Modern World Nations, Major World Cultures, Extreme Environments, and Global Connections series, he has a wonderful opportunity to combine each of these "hobbies." Dr. Gritzner has served as both president and executive director of the National Council for Geographic Education and has received the council's highest honor, the George J. Miller Award for Distinguished Service to Geographic Education, as well as other honors from the NCGE, Association of American Geographers, and other organizations.